WHAT ABOUT SCIENCE AND RELIGION?

A Study of Faith and Reason

FaithQuestions SERIES

Paul Stroble

for Clint McCann,
Thank you so much for your
beautiful commentary on
the Psalms,
which I cite on
pp. 110 and 111.

Paul Stroble

8/14

ABINGDON PRESS
NASHVILLE

WHAT ABOUT SCIENCE AND RELIGION?
A Study of Faith and Reason

This book is printed on acid-free, elemental chlorine-free paper.

ISBN: 978-0-687-64162-8

10 11 12 13 14 15—10 9 8 7 6 5 4 3

MANUFACTURED IN THE UNITED STATES OF AMERICA

CONTENTS

HOW TO USE
WHAT ABOUT SCIENCE AND RELIGION?
A STUDY OF FAITH AND REASON

WHAT ABOUT SCIENCE AND RELIGION? invites participants to consider ways to remain confident in their faith as they understand and appreciate the discoveries and advances of science. The book is designed for use in any of three settings: (1) adult Sunday school, (2) weekday adult groups, and (3) retreat settings. It can also provide a meaningful resource for private study and reflection.

Sunday School: WHAT ABOUT SCIENCE AND RELIGION? may be used on Sunday mornings as a short-term, seven-week study. Sunday morning groups generally last 45 to 60 minutes. If your group would like to go into greater depth, you can divide the chapters and do the study for longer than seven weeks.

Weekday Study: If you use WHAT ABOUT SCIENCE AND RELIGION? in a weekday study, we recommend 90-minute sessions. Participants should prepare ahead by reading the content of the chapter and choosing one activity for deeper reflection and study. A group leader may wish to assign these activities.

Retreat Study: You may wish to use WHAT ABOUT SCIENCE AND RELIGION? in a more intense study like a weekend retreat. Distribute the books at least two weeks in advance. Locate and provide additional media resources and reference materials, such as Bible dictionaries and commentaries, and a computer with Internet access. Tell participants to read WHAT ABOUT SCIENCE AND RELIGION? before the retreat begins. Begin on Friday with an evening meal or refreshments followed by gathering time and worship. Discuss the Introduction and Chapter 1. Cover Chapters 2, 3, 4, and 5 on Saturday, and Chapters 6 and 7 on Sunday. Develop a schedule that includes time for breaks, for meals, and for personal reflection of various topics in the chapters. End the retreat with closing worship on Sunday afternoon.

Leader/Learner Helps

Leader/learner helps are located in boxes near the relevant main text. They include a variety of discussion and reflection activities. Include both the Gathering and Closing worship activities in each session of your study, and choose from among the other leader/learner helps to fit the time frame you have chosen for your group.

The activities in the leader/learner helps meet the needs of a variety of personalities and ways of learning. They are designed to stimulate both solitary reflection and group discussion. An interactive and informal environment will foster a dynamic interchange of ideas and demonstrate the value of diverse perspectives. While the readings may be done in the group, reading outside of the session will enrich individual reflection and group discussion.

The Role of the Group Leader

A group leader facilitates gathering and closing worship, organizes the group for each session, monitors the use of time so that adequate attention is given to all major points of the chapter, and encourages an atmosphere of mutual respect and Christian caring. The leader should participate fully in the study as both learner and leader. The same person may lead all the sessions, or each session may have a different leader.

INTRODUCTION

Faith Seeking Understanding

Childhood is a time of discovery and exploration. For me, science played a big part of those joyful experiences. Born in the late 1950's, I grew up during a time when significant units of science education were introduced into public school curriculum. I recall studying simple versions of photosynthesis, astronomy, and zoology at my elementary school in Vandalia, Illinois. Our 1964 edition of the *World Book Encyclopedia* included science projects like making models of hydrogen and helium atoms from clear plastic balls. I used mason jars, but it was still a fun project.

I loved science! My favorite novel, *Henry Reed, Inc.*, was about a boy who did "pure and applied research" at his aunt and uncle's farm.[1] Children's books on dinosaurs, nature, and atoms stacked up on my bed; collections of rocks and butterflies became summertime hobbies. On my bedroom wall, I taped a large map of the planets, and I still remember the now-dated information thereon: Jupiter had 12 moons, Saturn nine, Pluto none. One summer, my parents bought me a chemistry set, which I enjoyed for a long time without blowing up the garage. Years later, in high school I took two years of chemistry and a year of physics with an exceptional teacher, Mr. Don Snyder.

Those were the days of drive-in B-movies that featured scientists who were misguided or "mad." Such clichés reflected an undercurrent of cultural anxiety about science: the pursuit of discovery, combined with human error or hubris, could have terrible results. Perhaps we didn't know how to use science properly. My favorite 1960's TV shows, *Lost in Space* and *The Time Tunnel*, were similarly premised; although the original *Star Trek*, another favorite, had a more hopeful vision. Most of all, those were the Cold War days—did we discover the secrets of the atom only to use those discoveries to destroy ourselves?

And yet the positive aspects of science remained. Science and scientists had made modern life better. People like Thomas Edison, Marie Curie, Albert Einstein, and Jonas Salk, among others, were cultural heroes, the subjects of children's books, people worthy to emulate.

When I took my first religion class in college, I appreciated the investigative method that certain theologians used to arrive at their conclusions. In these religious authors I saw a passion for truth and discovery. Generally speaking, theology, too, was subject to potential error, misuse, and human foolishness. But in a way I hadn't realized, theology was a science in the broad sense of the word, a way of understanding the world.

In my previous book in the *FaithQuestions* series, *What Do Other Faiths Believe?* (Abingdon Press, 2003), I show how Christians can understand and respect non-Christian beliefs without compromising their own faith-convictions. In this study, I show how Christians can remain confident in their faith while, at the same time, understanding and appreciating the discoveries and advances of science. We need not "give away" supernatural truth to naturalistic explanations, nor misrepresent and denigrate science in order to uphold Scripture.

As always I thank my family, Beth and Emily, my mother, Mildred Stroble, and also Odd Ball (*felis catus*), for their constant support and love. I also thank Chuck Barnes, Joel Green, Jim McClaren, John Green, David Wilkinson, and Rex Ramsier for their outstanding help, and Karen Allen for her expertise in fantasy and science fiction literature. None of these is responsible for my reflections, but their assistance has been indispensable. I also thank Pam Dilmore, editor of this series; Anna Raitt, production editor; Diana Hynson, who first guided me into church writing; and the team of *FaithLink*, an electronic curriculum piece for which I've written and researched many topics, including scientific ones, for over ten years.

Paul Stroble

---

[1] *Henry Reed, Inc.*, by Keith Robertson (The Viking Press, 1958); page 45.

CHAPTER 1
TWO KINDS OF TRUTH

Focus: This session introduces the relationship of science and religion. The two can be mutually exclusive, adversarial, or amiable.

Gathering

Introduce yourselves. Begin by going around the room and naming all the scientists of history that you can think of. Next, go around the room and name all the branches of science you can think of. How would you rate your own knowledge of science?

List all the questions you would like to consider in these lessons. Pray for God's guidance as you begin this study.

Who's Stronger?

You've seen those "fish" symbols on cars. The fish, which stands for Jesus, is a very ancient symbol of our Lord. If you take the first letters in the Greek phrase *Ieous Christos, Theou Uios, Sotier* (which means "Jesus Christ, Son of God, Savior"), you spell the Greek word for "fish," *ichthus*. Jesus' association with fishermen (Matthew 4:19) makes the symbol a meaningful one.

Several years ago I began to see a variation on that symbol. The fish had little feet, and inside the fish was the name "Darwin." The symbol obviously signifies Darwin's famous theory: the fish has evolved into an amphibian. I thought that was perversely clever but also bothersome. Is evolution, and more generally scientific theory, in competition with religion? Is the truth of science supposed to supersede "revealed truth"? Does science replace Jesus as Savior?

> How did Jesus "catch" you? Did you become a Christian as a child or as an adult? What questions do you still struggle with as you grow spiritually?

Then I saw a different symbol on the Internet: a Darwin fish being swallowed by a Jesus fish, along with the caption, "Survival of the Fittest." That bothered me more. Is religious belief supposed to be an enemy of evolutionary theory? By implication, is Jesus the foe of scientific inquiry? Plus, isn't "survival of the fittest" an objectionable idea for many people?

As I worked on this chapter, my teenage daughter saw a book that lay beside my computer. "'Religion and Science'?" she asked, repeating the title. "That's a weird combination!" She revealed a feeling that many of us have: the two fields seem to be two kinds of truth, difficult to reconcile and perhaps even rivals.

> Science and technology are different, though interrelated, terms. Science is the study of a variety of subjects—medicine, biology, genetics, physics, and so on—often resulting in products and machines that enhance our lives. Technology has to do with the applications of science. In anthropology, technology refers to the tools that humans make. An arrowhead is technology, as is a space probe. But today, most technology comes from scientific research and development, rather than hand-crafted production.

Ubiquitous Science

As kids would say, "Science rules!"[1] Can you think of aspects of your life that aren't affected by science, or by the technological results of science? I can't. Each day I benefit from science: the purified and fluoridated tap water that I drink, the medicine that I take, the many machines that I use, and so on. I might have died in childhood (like, for instance, six of my grandmother's siblings many years ago) if not for the antibiotics and inoculations that I took when very young. I'm grateful for the many scientific discoveries that make life safer and better. I'm also grateful for the ability of science to warn us about potential troubles, such as environmental crises and ethical issues that emerge from medical discoveries.

"Modernity" is a word given to several interrelated aspects of our contemporary world: democratic and representative governments; technological and industrial economies; broad equality and rights among people; the freedom of scientific inquiry; and in many countries, freedom of religious expression. Although science and technology have greatly benefited the modern world, observers note the "downsides" to technology: more sophisticated weaponry, environmental challenges, and a secularism that some believe undercuts religious values. Thus, modernity brings both new opportunities and insecurities.

Alvin Toffler, in his famous book from 1970, *Future Shock*, divides human history into approximately 800 lifetimes. He notes that only in the last 70 lifetimes have human beings had written language; only in the last six lifetimes have we had printed language; and only in the 800th lifetime have we had the products and appliances that we rely upon daily. Little wonder that we feel insecure sometimes! He also notes that modern science has progressed stupendously, but without the feeling of us having arrived at a good place.[2]

Centuries ago, science and theology went hand-in-hand since they were founded upon similar philosophical principles. But this is no longer the case. Modern science operates by human observation, reason, and research rather than religious doctrines and sacred scriptures. Scientists themselves can be atheists or deeply religious, as they choose.

In spite of the predominant influence of science and technology, religion shows no sign of abating its influence in our modern era. Some of the religious fervor in our world is, unfortunately, scary and dangerous. But sincere people continue to find not only solace in religious belief but also positive life-changes, deep purpose, and divine help. Many of us can point to specific instances in our lives when God intervened decisively in our lives. Though God is not an object of scientific proof and investigation, people of faith do not doubt the existence and activity of God.

> Discuss your "gut feelings" about science. Is it (1) fascinating and important; (2) something you really don't understand; (3) a scary, risky thing; (4) a mixed blessing?

Thus many of us balance our religious certainties with the certainties of science, and we're not sure how these certainties can be reconciled, if at all. What are ways that science and religion interrelate?

Religion Trumps Science

It seems that on one hand, religious truths "trump" scientific truths. For instance, I believe in the Virgin Birth, the resurrection of Jesus, and the eventual resurrection of the dead. I believe that Jesus will return someday. From a strictly scientific viewpoint, these ideas are unprovable and even impossible; yet from the viewpoint of faith they are true.

Think about the meaning of the gospel of Jesus. It is salvation and eternal life (John 3:16), a mortal blow against powers of evil (1 Corinthians 15:24-28), the defeat of sin and death (1 Corinthians 15:51-57), reconciliation with God (Romans 5:10-11), mercy and grace from God (Romans 6:23; Hebrews 4:16), confidence in approaching God (Hebrews 4:15-16), assurance that God will never forsake us (Romans 8:31-39), gentleness from God (Hebrews 5:2), freedom from being "good enough to please God" (Romans 3:21-26), power for living (1 Corinthians 4:20; 1 Thessalonians 1:5), power for growth (Galatians 5:22-23), freedom from anxiety (Philippians 4:6), the peace which is even better than "peace of mind" (Philippians 4:7), and many other wonderful things!

As you look up some of these references, which are particularly meaningful to you?

Read together 1 Corinthians 1:18-25. What would "wisdom of the world" be from Paul's viewpoint? What would be twenty-first-century "wisdom of the world"?

Some people believe that stories in Genesis 1–2 give specific, historical truth about the creation of the world. God created the world in six days, several thousand years ago. God created the species, although species do alter over time, but not contrary to God's specific plan. Even if you don't read Genesis literally, you may believe in the basic truths of the account: God's establishment of the light from darkness, God's creation of the cosmos, the diversification of the species, and the dominion given to man and woman—all by God's word, creative power, and care. I also believe in God's ongoing, tender, and detailed care of creation as depicted in Psalm 104. The creativeness and the providence of God are truths that are not scientific, in that we know these truths by faith.

Many of us can point to instances in our lives when God worked miracles: a sickness healed, a hopeless situation fixed, a loved one converted.

I can point to situations in my life where God worked mightily. Again, none of these are scientific truths, and some of them could be explained in a non-religious way. Examples of God's care in my life could simply be explained as serendipity, chance, or me "making my own good luck." Nevertheless, we believe these kinds of miracles are true.

Paul contrasts religion with, if not science specifically, the wisdom of the world; and the world's wisdom pales in comparison to the truth of the cross. "Has not God made foolish the wisdom of the world? For since, in the wisdom of God, the world did not know God through wisdom, God decided, through the foolishness of our proclamation, to save those who believe" (1 Corinthians 1:20b-21). The truth of Christ crucified is better than human wisdom and strength (verse 25).

Thus, religious truth seems to supersede the wisdom of human beings. Science, by its nature, does not deal with supernatural truths. But, you might say, so much the worse for science; supernatural truths are those we need for eternal life!

Science an Enemy?

Religion and science are often portrayed as opponents, with science on the "bad side." Many conservative Christians, for instance, perceive an erosion of values in this country. They worry that science, especially evolutionary theory, contributes to an anti-religious secularization of contemporary society.

As I worked on this book during the fall of 2005, issues of public education and medical research filled the news. During that autumn, the school board in Dover, Pennsylvania, near Harrisburg, voted to include intelligent design in ninth grade biology curriculum as another explanation to the origins of life. But a federal judge ruled that the board had acted unconstitutionally; intelligent design, the judge

> Do you agree that science is an aspect of a burgeoning secularization in the U.S.? Why or why not?

maintained, is a religious idea connected with Christianity and therefore not suitable for a science class.[3] The nonprofit Christian law firm that handled the case aimed to help "'change the culture'" in the U.S. by pressing the cause of intelligent design. In fact, an attorney in the Dover case said at the time that "there is an attempt to slowly remove every symbol of Christianity and religious faith in our country."[4]

The debate of whether alternative theories like intelligent design should be taught along side of, or instead of, evolution will surely go on many years; for many people think that religion has been pushed out of educational curriculum in favor of an "atheistic" theory, evolution. Science seems to them an enemy of biblical truth.

Hot-button issues, such as stem-cell research, cloning, right-to-life debates, and others, raise concerns. Should human embryonic cells be grown in the laboratory in order to help persons suffering from various illnesses? Is genetic research a suitable pursuit, even though it promises new treatment for disease? Perhaps scientific research encroaches into ethically uncertain areas without concern for consequences. To some people, science undercuts traditional values.

Science Trumps Religion

Let's look at the issue from another angle. There are instances where religion seems reactionary and foolish compared to the progress and advancements of science.

According to popular thinking, many people believed the world was flat. During the Middle Ages, when science and theology went hand-in-hand, erroneous ideas about the universe prevailed. But (again, according to a popular perception) once science became freed from religious constraints, scientists used human reason to discover key truths about the universe.

One famous case, which we'll also consider later, is that of Galileo. As the story goes, the Church condemned Galileo because his scientific theories contradicted Christian doctrine. Galileo's science was correct, even though the church forced him to be dishonest and deny the truth. Galileo became a martyr for the integrity of science in the face of anti-intellectual, authoritarian religion. (I discuss this case in more detail in Chapter 5.)

The "Scopes monkey trial" is another example. John Scopes was tried in 1925 for teaching evolution in his high school class, contrary to Tennessee law. He was convicted and fined, but the case made headlines and actually helped the cause of science. The Tennessee law was eventually overturned by the U.S. Supreme Court as violating church-state separation.

Read about the Scopes trial at http://www.law.umkc.edu/faculty/projects/FTrials/scopes/scopes.htm. Then watch the movie *Inherit the Wind*, which dramatizes (with license) the trial.

More recently, the "culture wars" in the U.S. have, in the minds of many, hurt the cause of science. One observer worries that school boards that push intelligent design over evolution are actually "violating the integrity of science" and "confusing the students not only about what is science, but confusing them about what is religion."[5] In this view, religious people, unintentionally or willfully, misrepresent the claims of science in order to pursue a religious and social agenda.

"Science requires an open mind, free inquiry, critical thinking, the willingness to question assumptions, and peer review," notes author Paul Kurtz. "The test of a theory or hypothesis is independent . . . of bias, prejudice, faith, or tradition; and it is justified by the evidence, logical consistency, and mathematical coherence." Religions, on the other hand, "rely on the acceptance of faith in specific revelations and their interpretation by differing prophets, priests, ministers, rabbis, monks, or mullahs."[6] In other words, religion lacks the rigor and openness of science. Science is self-correcting, but religion merely requires acquiescence. Religion is biased, while science relies upon peer review, logical consistence, and constant questioning of assumptions. This is a one-sided view of religion, as I will discuss in Chapter 2, but some scientists do hold to this view.

An Amiable Relation

Now let's look at the issue from yet another angle. Ian Barbour, professor emeritus of physics and religion at Carleton College, sees four broad ways that religion and science relate to each other: conflict, independence, dialogue, and integration. He shows how these relationships function in several areas of science and religion in his book, *When Science Meets Religion: Enemies, Strangers, or Partners?* (HarperCollins Publishers, 2000).

Even those of us with very conservative interpretations of Scripture tend to pick and choose which Bible passages we take literally and which we do not. Most of us no longer regard people as demon-possessed (Mark 1:21-28). We no longer believe that all "drunkenness" (Galatians 5:21) is a moral failure; we now know that some

> The term "hermeneutical" means principles for interpreting a text—in this case the Bible. What is your "hermeneutic"? Are there Bible passages that you cannot interpret literally? If not, how do you decide what in the Bible is literally true and what is symbolically true or culturally outmoded?

people have a physiological intolerance for alcohol and can be treated. We feel uncomfortable as we read stories in the Book of Joshua that seem to justify war and extermination. We no longer consider adultery and rebelliousness in children as capital crimes (Deuteronomy 21:18-21; 22:22), nor that women should keep silent in church (1 Corinthians 14:33b-36), nor that sickness is the result of sin and God's anger (Psalm 38:1-4). In these cases and others, modern thinking has "updated" the worldview of the biblical authors. Consequently, we must make prayerful decisions how we interpret Scripture.

We rely upon God during medical emergencies, but prayer is not the only thing we do; we also consult physicians, trusting that they are skilled in the best and latest science of healing. We're thankful for medical discoveries that have nearly eradicated once-feared diseases like polio. We place our hope and trust in ongoing scientific breakthroughs that will someday provide cures for cancer, AIDS, spinal injuries, and other fearful conditions.

Many religious people are comfortable with theories such as evolution, the "Big Bang," or the geological antiquity of the earth. They accept the discoveries of science and the cogency of the scientific method. They marvel at astronomical discoveries and the vastness of the universe. But at the same time, these people maintain the essential truths of the Bible: God has created and continues to sustain the world and is accomplishing God's plans of salvation. Science may not prove God's existence but it uncovers amazing aspects of the world that we call God's.

> At your grocery or bookstore, browse through magazines like *Discovery*, *Scientific American*, *Seed*, *Astronomy*, and others. Find articles about science that interest you.

Certainly not all scientists are atheists. Dan R. Dick, a United Methodist writer on discipleship topics, notes,

> The majority of scientists I read and speak to admit that they wrestle constantly with issues of faith. I have corresponded with hundreds of scientists who are Christian and I am amazed at the number of religious leaders who are well versed and well read in various disciplines of science. This is not now, and never has been, an "either/or" debate, though the most vocal proponents on both sides attempt to make it so.[8]

In the passage from 1 Corinthians 1, quoted earlier, Paul is not condemning the wisdom of the world per se. His purpose is to heal divisions in the church (1:10-12); for the Corinthians were easily impressed by big, bold signs of wisdom, power, and influence. Rather than condemning the wisdom of the world, Paul counsels the church to keep things in perspective: God has chosen the foolishness of the cross to bring salvation, so there is no excuse for factions and quarrels.

> Look up Psalm 19:1-4. How do the world and heavens "speak" of God? How does the universe speak of God's love? How does one hear the "voices" of the world? Read the rest of the psalm. What are other ways we know God?

David Wilkinson, a British Methodist minister, writer, and professor at St. Johns College, University of Durham, has written many books and articles on issues of faith and science. He decries the "'science-bashing'" in which many Christians engage and urges that Christians become educated in science and support scientists.[9] "Christian ministry," he says, "is also exercised by scientists, medics, teachers, technologists, engineers and others who explore or use the regularities of the Universe."[10] He writes that, during a Methodist service he attended in Ireland,

> the minister did something in the prayers of intercession that struck me as quite unusual. He simply prayed for scientists who had to make difficult decisions. At that point I remembered talking to a scientist at the forefront of medical research, bringing a Christian witness to questions of deep complexity, who said to me, 'I sometimes wish my church prayed for me just occasionally with the fervor that we pray for overseas missionaries.'[11]

Are Americans Ambivalent About Science?

In addition to supporting scientists with our prayers and finances, we need to deepen our understanding of science and its methods. Ambivalence toward science seems to be common among a portion of Americans.

Americans are partly ambivalent about science because of contemporary cultural issues. Dr. John C. Green, director of the Ray C. Bliss Institute of Applied Politics at the University of Akron, recently spoke with me. "Americans are deeply divided over abortion," he says, "but lately the debate has spilled over to issues like stem-cell research, environmental

> Have you read the book *Jurassic Park*, by Michael Crichton (Knopf, 1990), or have you seen the movie? The story (with obvious Frankenstein overtones) concerns dinosaurs that have been cloned from fossilized DNA by scientists who have exploited the discovery without considering the consequences. Do you think that's a fair portrayal of scientific research? Why or why not?

protection, biology teaching in public schools, and others. Possibly these issues might not be discussed so intensely if they were examined on their own merits, but because of the larger political and cultural issues in the U.S., people respond to these issues more passionately. Someone already upset about abortion, for instance, may have a strong response about stem cells."

Jim Holt, writing in the *New York Times*, notes:

> Science is the distinctive achievement and crowning glory of the modern age. . . . It is also something that, relatively speaking, the United States is pretty good at. . . . Oddly, though, Americans on the whole do not seem to care greatly for science. . . . Only one in five has bothered to take a physics course. Three out of four haven't heard that the universe is expanding. . . . Less than ten percent of adult Americans, it is estimated, are in possession of basic scientific literacy. This ignorance of science, flecked with outright hostility, is worth pondering at a moment when three of the nation's most contentious political issues—global warming, stem-cell research and the teaching of intelligent design—are scientific in character.[12]

> One writer complains that religious people tend to be "labeled" whenever they raise questions about science. For instance, people concerned about stem-cell research are tagged "anti-abortionists" or "conservatives."[13] Do you think this true? Start watching your newspaper or favorite news magazines for stories about religion and science. How is science portrayed? How are religious people portrayed? What are the typical issues discussed?

For similar reasons, funding for scientific research has been declining in recent years. A recent issue of *Time* (February 13, 2006) noted the decreasing levels of investment and innovation in science in the U.S., compared to other countries.[14] Robert Hemenway, chancellor of the University of Kansas, said in 2005 that "our focus should be to raise the level of scientific literacy among our citizenry because we face a critical shortage of scientists in the next two decades."[15]

As the saying goes, the pendulum swings from one extreme to another. Perhaps in the near future, anxieties about science will give way to a renewed appreciation among Americans. Books like *Chasing Science: Science as Spectator Sport*, by Frederik Pohl (Tor Books, 2003), and others communicate some of the enjoyment and wonder that people can experience by exploring science.

What This Book Is About

In this book I look at several of the issues involved in the science and religion debate. I discuss the meaning of scientific and religious truth, the traditional relationship of faith and reason, evolutionary theory, astronomy, modern medical research, and the ways that we read Scripture in our scientific age. I also recommend a variety of books, with widely different viewpoints, in order for you to increase your knowledge. Altogether, I hope to clarify aspects of both of these wonderful fields.

Religious people can understand and appreciate scientific discoveries while remaining confident about their own truth convictions. We unintentionally do harm to religion when we attack science without properly understanding its methods and discoveries. Relying upon caricatures and slogans (including Scripture verses used as discussion-ending slogans) does not advance the cause of our faith. But we also do harm to religion when we try too much to accommodate it to science and place a rationalistic "spin" on religious beliefs, as Kenneth Miller puts it, "trying to find a way of apologizing religious belief into scientific fact."[16]

"For all things are yours, whether Paul or Apollos or Cephas or the world or life or death or the present or the future—all belong to you, and you belong to Christ, and Christ belongs to God" (1 Corinthians 3:21b-23). The theologian Paul Tillich has a classic sermon on this text. For Tillich, we need not fear science or other aspects of the wisdom of the world, insofar as we belong to Christ. Christ sets us free so that, among other things, we can appreciate and use the wisdom of the world without fear. But at the same time, the wisdom of the world can never know Christ and the freedom he gives us to love and serve one another.[17] *That* wisdom comes from God—and praise be to God, who has claimed us with steadfast love (Romans 8:31).

Closing
Pray together Psalm 104:24, 33-34: "O LORD, how manifold are your works! In wisdom you have made them all; the earth is full of your creatures.... I will sing to the LORD as long as I live; I will sing praise to my God while I have being. May my meditation be pleasing to him, for I rejoice in the LORD."

For Further Reading
The Hidden Face of God: How Science Reveals the Ultimate Truth, by Gerald L. Schroeder (Touchstone, 2001).

Science and Religion: Are They Compatible? edited by Paul Kurtz (Prometheus Books, 2003).

Science and Theology: An Introduction, by John Polkinghorne (Augsburg Fortress, 1998).

When Science Meets Religion: Enemies, Strangers, or Partners? by Ian G. Barbour (HarperCollins, 2000).

Notes

[1] "Science rules!" is a phrase featured at the opening of the children's show *Bill Nye the Science Guy*, which ran on PBS from 1993–2002.

[2] *Future Shock*, by Alvin Toffler (Random House, 1970); pages 12–17.

[3] From "Intelligent Design Flunked," by Lisa Anderson, in the *Chicago Tribune*, December 21, 2005; available at: http://www.chicagotribune.com/news/nationworld/-chi-0512210296dec21,0,6748957.story.

[4] From "In Intelligent Design Case, a Cause in Search of a Lawsuit," by Laurie Goodstein, in the *New York Times*, November 4, 2005.

[5] From "In Kansas, Teaching Biology Is Survival of Fittest," by Lisa Anderson, in the *Chicago Tribune*, December 30, 2005; available at: http://www.chicagotribune.com/-news/nationworld/chi-0512300277dec30,0,6355740.story.

[6] *Science and Religion: Are They Compatible?* edited by Paul Kurtz (Prometheus Books, 2003); page 13. Mostly critical of religion, this book contains excellent essays from noted scientists concerning the science-religion conflict.

[8] "Facing the Wrong Way—God, Darwin, and Being Too Smart for Our Own Good," by Dan R. Dick; accessible from the website of the General Board of Discipleship of The United Methodist Church at: http://www.gbod.org/TextOnly.asp?item_id=8729.

[9] From "The Christian Value of Science," by Dr. David Wilkinson, in the *Methodist Recorder*, November 1999.

[10] From "Is It Holier to Be a Methodist Minister Than a Scientist?" by Dr. David Wilkinson, in the *Methodist Recorder*, March 2000.

[11] See note 9 above.

[12] "The Way We Live Now: 12-11-05; Madness About a Method," by Jim Holt, in the *New York Times*, December 11, 2005.

[13] From "Biotech Debates Are Being Muddled by the Media," by Daniel McConchie, for the Center for Bioethics and Human Dignity, April 5, 2001; accessible at: http://www.cbhd.org/resources/biotech/mcconchie_2001-04-05_print.htm.

[14] "Are We Losing Our Edge?" by Michael D. Lemonick, in *Time*, Vol. 167, No. 7, February 13, 2006; pages 22–33.

[15] From a statement issued by Robert E. Hemenway, chancellor of University of Kansas; accessible at: http://www.kuconnection.org/2005oct/news_4.asp.

[16] *Finding Darwin's God: A Scientist's Search for Common Ground Between God and Evolution*, by Kenneth R. Miller (Harper Perennial, 2000); page 258.

[17] *The New Being*, by Paul Tillich (Charles Scribner's Sons, 1955); pages 110 13.

CHAPTER 2
WHAT IS SCIENCE?
WHAT IS RELIGION?

Focus: This session examines the truth-claims and methods of science and religion.

Gathering
Greet one another. Read Proverbs 8:22-31. "Wisdom" is the speaker in this passage. How is wisdom related to the natural world? Then read Proverbs 4:1-9. Is this a different kind of wisdom? How are the two passages related? Pray for God's presence and guidance to be with you during this session exploring the truth claims and methods of religion and science.

What's the Difference?

In Chapter 1, we looked briefly at the varied relationships between science and religion. Let us now take a little more in-depth look at the two fields.

My friend Chuck Barnes, a retired geologist, is a long-time member of a church I once served as an associate pastor. When I asked him for his thoughts about this project, he promptly wrote me a long letter with his reflections about science and faith, which I revisit throughout this book. "Science and faith," he told me, "are, in a way, simply different expressions of what it means to be human. They ask quite different sets of questions and have quite different views of *what counts* as 'evidence.'"

How do you respond to the idea of science and religion as "complementary ways of understanding"?

Chuck Barnes continues, "If people insist on seeing science and religious faith as polar opposites, then people will argue that each defames the other. This last point of view is one with which I am in *total disagreement*. Notice that I said that science and religion are 'different expressions.' I didn't say they were opposites; rather, they are complementary ways of understanding."

Find a copy of *The Essential Dictionary of Science*, edited by John O. E. Clark (Barnes and Noble, 2004). Find a quiet time and place and then browse through the book at random. Do you know many of the terms and theories described in the book? Dip into the dictionary as you pursue this study. You may also find helpful *The Complete Idiot's Guide® to Theories of the Universe*, by Gary F. Moring (Alpha, 2002), which includes both scientific and religious theories.

What Is Science?

Science is a disciplined and rigorous way of understanding the natural world in all its glories. We may think of scientists as people in lab coats in rooms full of test tubes. But "science" is a rubric covering many different fields: biology, zoology, physics, chemistry, astronomy, medicine, paleontology, and many others.

Chuck Barnes writes, "Science is reasoned experience seeking understanding of the *material* world. These understandings are not about issues of purpose or meaning, but rather issues of processes and interactions, *how things work*. These are the truths that come largely from reason, experiment, and experience—truths that form the body of tentative knowledge termed science."

Science is "tentative" knowledge not because it is slipshod or insecure, but because science remains open to new discoveries. Even the most secure and proven theory could, potentially at least, be challenged by a new discovery.

Scientific Method: Making Hypotheses

The scientific method is a process of observation, description, and creation of hypotheses and theories. Let's say I am an ornithologist and discover a bird with which I'm unfamiliar. I make a hypothesis that this is a new species. But I must thoroughly study the bird's characteristics, compare it with known species, and discuss my findings with other scientists. Or, I am a chemist seeking a cure for a disease. After many experiments I discover a chemical compound that seems to work. But I must continue to test it for its effectiveness and safety.

A hypothesis is a premise to be tested. It may or may not be a true hypothesis; but for now, it's a plausible conclusion, based on the available evidence. Now, however, it must be tested by ongoing observations and experiments. Experiments and ongoing study are essential in the scientific process.

> The Bible speaks of "testing" in a moral and spiritual rather than a scientific kind of way. A "test" can be a temptation or a "trial," or an attitude toward God. Look up Malachi 3:10; Matthew 22:18; and 1 Peter 1:6-7. What kinds of tests and trials are found in these verses? Can you think of any other biblical examples? How are spiritual tests analogous to scientific/empirical tests?

Scientific Method: Developing Theories

How about theories? People often think the word "theory" means the same as hypothesis. Actually, a theory is a hypothesis that has stood up under many experiments and is now a framework or model for understanding phenomena. Even more, a theory provides a framework for the discovery of new phenomena and observations.

Good theories explain more phenomena than initially anticipated. For instance, Einstein's famous formula, $E=mc^2$, was developed years before scientists knew how to "split the atom" and use atomic energy, but his formula explained well why so much energy derives from a very small amount of matter.[1]

Even the best theories require refinement. For instance, Newton's theory of gravity is an excellent theory. Gravity happens. But Newton's calculations, which

> What was your science education? How much science do you know now? How much science do you use now?

explained most phenomena, did not explain discrepancies in the orbit of the planet Mercury. The theory needed additional insight—in this case, Einstein's theory that space and time are also affected by gravity. Using

Einstein's principles, scientists could correctly calculate Mercury's orbit, which is affected by the sun's strong gravity.[2]

According to the Ptolemaic theory of the solar system, the sun and planets orbited the earth. His theory was wrong in the sense that it was superseded by the Copernican model. But in a way, that theory was true in that it was useful; it suitably explained phenomena as they were observable *at the time*.[4]

Even very sound theories could be superseded someday, if future evidence comes in. The pursuit of scientific knowledge is always open to new observations, new evidence, and new possibilities. It is a very honest pursuit!

I emphasize this because you hear people dismissively say, "Evolutionary theory is full of holes," or "Global warming is just a theory." Scientific theories *are* subject to ongoing testing, and there *are* gaps in many scientific theories. But "gaps" simply means that human understanding is ongoing. If we do not agree with a theory, we should do so honestly, without misrepresenting the meaning of scientific inquiry.

Here are a few examples[3] of contemporary scientific theories:

Evolution: the theory that species change gradually over time, including the theory that complex species have developed from ancient, single-celled organisms. This theory is foundational for modern biology.

Quantum mechanics: the theory that energy can be measured in multiples of units called quanta and that subatomic particles can also behave like waves. The theory is foundational for particle physics as well as the physics of silicon chips.

Relativity: the theory that time and space are interdependent and also relative to the speed of light. The theory is foundational for cosmology and astrophysics.

Plate tectonics: the theory that the earth's outer layer consists of shifting plates. The theory is foundational for geology and seismology.

Greenhouse effect: First predicted in 1827, it is the theory that certain gases like carbon dioxide, water vapor, methane, and others trap the sun's heat and warm the earth. This is also the theory that underlies the observation of global warming.

Is Science Neutral?

Experiments should be as "neutral" as possible. For instance, a scientist should be open to whatever data comes

> What kind of problem solver are you? Do you like to find solutions to difficult situations? Do you prefer that others solve your problems for you?

from an experiment. Having several people working separately on the same project, and publishing in peer-reviewed journals, helps to eliminate bias. Mistakes can happen in experiments; so independent verification by multiple experimenters can help eliminate error. I remember working with a classmate in my high school chemistry class; my friend and I checked each other's work, which made for greater accuracy. Occasionally we hear stories of scientists who "fudge" research, but such fraud is not very widespread.

Research always includes failed experiments, incorrect hypotheses, and fresh starts. In recent years, science stories have tremendously increased in newspapers and news magazines, while foreign-affairs coverage has decreased.[5] The media frequently reports research findings as if they are definitive. This leaves the everyday person confused. Are certain foods healthy or not? Are certain dietary supplements helpful or not? Are fossil discoveries definitively identified or not?

An *Associated Press* story reported on scientific research concerning whether humans and chimps had offspring together over six million years ago. But in scientific theory, genus *Homo* did not appear until about two million years ago, and *Homo sapiens*

> What reports about scientific research have been confusing to you? How?

did not appear until a half-million years ago. (Chimps are genus *Pan*.) The study centered on ancient antecedent species, but the news story uses the modern terms "human and chimp." A good knowledge of science helps us to read news reports critically.[6]

Scientific data can be challenging even to other scientists! One researcher examined data about mental problems and substance abuse among homeless people; but among the eighty studies that the researcher found, the findings were too different to be helpful.[7] Working with a colleague, a friend of mine starting out in the medical field has researched numerous articles about the quality-of-life issues faced by patients on anti-HIV medication. Research in the biomedical sciences can be overwhelming; over two million medical articles are published around the world every year. Research in the social sciences, where human subjects may respond in varying ways, can lead to complicated results.[8]

Some writers portray science as a cool-headed search for truth, always self-correcting and rational. Actually, university politics, competition for research funding, and desire for recognition are also factors within the scientific community. Many scientists are under tremendous pressure to publish their findings, and the most notable findings are those that challenge or correct previous studies.[9] Some scientific topics are highly politicized—global warming, stem-cell research, atomic energy, endangered species, and other issues are discussed and debated not only within the scientific community but also as social and political issues. In a free and open society, this kind of controversy is inevitable.

Method, Philosophy, and Politics

> Have you ever had experiences where church seemed very political? What happened? How did you respond?

Science will always *seem* at odds with religion because of its method. Science is a methodologically materialistic enterprise, that is, it uses only natural explanations. (In this sense, "materialistic" means limited to the physical world.)[10] Science does not address questions of "why" something happens: for instance, why the universe exists. Rather, science addresses "how" questions and finds the answers in observable, testable data. Dr. John C. Green, director of the Ray C. Bliss Institute of Applied Politics at the University of Akron, notes that "non-theistic scientists want to assign meaning and purpose in life to natural processes, while religious people want to assign meaning and purpose to God. To the extent that people inform their self-understanding by these notions, serious conflicts can develop."

Philosophy can also put science and religion at odds. There is a philosophical distinction between science and scientism. Scientism is the idea that scientific explanations are the *only* explanations possible for anything.[11]

This philosophy is also called reductionism. Epistemological reductionism means that all true knowledge is gained by scientific inquiry. A person with this philosophy may not deny religious doctrines but will

> How do you respond to the idea that all true knowledge is gained by scientific inquiry?

deny that we have any valid knowledge of the reality of those doctrines. Such doctrines remain in the realm of faith, opinion, poetry, and so on.[12]

Theodore Drange, retired philosopher at Cornell, questions whether scientists who are also religious are inherently inconsistent, since part of the scientific method is to assume that, eventually, all phenomena can be explained in terms of natural laws. But if a miracle is explained by natural laws, it's no longer a miracle! A scientist who believes in the possibility of miracles seems to be compartmentalizing his or her science and religion.[14] Chuck Barnes disagrees, saying that, in scientific method, while all *natural* phenomena is subject to investigation and can be explained by natural laws, this does not apply to "all phenomena."

> Here are some examples of scientism[13]:
>
> "The Cosmos is all that is or ever was or ever will be."—*Carl Sagan*
>
> "Man knows at last that he is alone in the universe's unfeeling immensity, out of which he emerged only by chance." —*Jacques Monod*
>
> "It may not be too much to say that sociology and the other social sciences, as well as the humanities, are the last branches of biology to be included in the Modern Synthesis." (In other words, even the arts, and also religion, are part of what Wilson calls "'the neural machinery of the brain.'")—*Edward O. Wilson*

> What feelings or thoughts occur to you as you consider the notion that not all phenomena can be explained by natural laws?

Another kind of philosophy, metaphysical reductionism (or metaphysical materialism), denies that God and spiritual reality exist. Thus the only reality that exists is physical reality, which can be examined by science—matter and energy.[15]

Ian Barbour, a well-known author on these issues, notes that theism (the belief in God) "is not inherently in conflict with science, but it does conflict with a metaphysics of materialism."[16] Scientists do make philosophical claims, he writes, but when they use science to, for instance, deny God's existence, they are overreaching the proper realm of science.[17]

> Read the article "Science—Friend or Foe?" by Denis R. Alexander, originally published in the *Cambridge Paper* series in September 1995.[18]

29

Politics is another area in which religion and science seem at odds. John Green of the Bliss Institute explained it to me well:

> Conflicts between science and religion become serious politically when the coercive power of the government comes into play. One issue is regulations. Polls show that many scientists are religious, and I've never met a scientist who didn't believe in appropriate regulations. But scientists bristle when they see religious standards being applied to regulate scientific activity. Another issue is the teaching of evolutionary biology in public schools. Still another issue is the application of ethics and morals, as, for instance, in end of life issues. I do not see an inherent conflict between religion and science, but there are actual conflicts, for instance in these issues where politics come into play.

What Is Religion?

Now let us look at religion. Chuck Barnes writes,

> Science seeks those truths that come from reason applied to observation of the *material*, physical world. Theology, in contrast, seeks those truths that come from reflection, prayer, and divine revelation about the *immaterial* world. Science deals with issues like 'How does this work?' 'Of what is this made?' 'How is it made?' Theology deals with issues of 'Who are we?' 'Why are we here?' 'What is our purpose?'

Religion has to do with ultimate reality (God, heavenly beings, the afterlife, etc.) and the beliefs and practices that relate to ultimate reality (ways to worship, ethics, patterns of personal devotion, social responsibilities, etc.). There are numerous religions in the world with different conceptions of God and worship. Although religions of the world share many common beliefs, they also differ in "non-negotiables." Either you believe the Koran is God's word, or you don't; either you believe Jesus is God's Son, or you don't; either you believe in karma and reincarnation, or you don't. We can learn from other religions' beliefs, but eventually we must make a decision and declare our allegiance to one faith.

A Different Kind of Evidence

But we do base our faith upon evidence. When we place our faith in God, we are doing something more than holding to an informed opinion.

For instance, I prefer one political party to another because of convictions and preference. Belief and faith are inseparable from God's grace. God initiates and sustains a relationship with us. God provides us wonderful help, including evidence.

A person I once knew wanted proof of God, so he wished out loud (testing God, in a way) that he could find a four-leaf clover. The person had never, ever found a four-leaf clover. This time he found several. Such proof would not stand up under the scrutiny of a reductionist examination; the man's experience resulted from chance or psychological suggestion. Faith, however, gives a "why" explanation: the man needed to know something about God, and God met the man "where he was" in order to start him on a faith relationship.

Another way that Christians deal with evidence is the evidence of a person's life. The witness of a trusted person is an important "proof" of religious truth. As Alister McGrath points out, a person might not have any problem addressing difficult intellectual challenges to faith, such as the problem of evil. But that same person might experience a faith crisis when encountering a hypocritical Christian leader, for instance, who preaches against certain sins while practicing those same sins.[19]

> Reflect upon your own faith journey. What kind of evidence has helped your Christian faith? What kinds of experiences hurt your faith? When your faith was hurt, was the reason perhaps disappointing events in your life, a seemingly unanswered prayer, or religious people who let you down?

How would you defend your faith if you were questioned? What evidence would you give to prove the truth of your faith—and to lead others to that truth?

Read Mark 4:35-41. Why don't the disciples understand this evidence about Jesus? When are times that we, too, are slow to understand evidence?

Chuck Barnes puts it this way:

> Beliefs are something we are; they are not something we *have*. If you tell me that you believe in God and then continue to act in an uncaring fashion, I will eventually argue that you do not truly believe what you say you do. In a mature Christian, beliefs lead to a particular lifestyle and the ability to share those beliefs with others in an understandable way. Belief systems are not wholly irrational, though the evidence one uses to defend/explain them is commonly founded on reflection, prayer, and revelation—all quite personal experiences. So non-believers may perceive our faith as irrational.

31

Some science authors portray religion as an anti-intellectual assent to authorities, whether a scriptural book, an ordained teacher, or a probably punitive assembly of clergy.[20] Actually, religion is a closely studied field with academic respectability and numerous fields of inquiry. Magazines like the *Christian Century* and *Christianity Today* follow religious trends. Academic journals, such as *Journal of Religion, Journal of Biblical Literature, Journal of the American Academy of Religion*, and many others, contain peer-reviewed articles based upon research and investigation. Research in religion is more closely related to the social sciences than the natural and technological sciences, though religion speaks to these as well.

> In what ways do you understand the statement that beliefs are something we are rather than something we have? What illustrations from life illuminate this statement?

Some scientific writers are harsh critics of religion. Daniel C. Dennett, for instance, believes that religion is a natural phenomenon. (See his books *Darwin's Dangerous Idea* (Simon & Schuster, 1996) and *Breaking the Spell* (Viking, 2006).) Richard Dawkins, in *The Selfish Gene* (Oxford University Press, 1976), argues that altruism, as well as competition, can be explained by our genes. Edward O. Wilson, in *Sociobiology: The New Synthesis* (Belknap Press, 2000), and Robert Wright, in *The Moral Animal* (Vintage, 1994), also apply evolutionary theory to naturalistic explanations of human behavior.

Sam Harris, in his book *The End of Faith: Religion, Terror, and the Future of Reason* (W.W. Norton &. Co., 2004), criticizes religion—specifically the unreasonable posture of faith that, he argues, leads to inhumanity, intolerance, and violence. But reason and evidence lead to opposite effects: cooperation and tolerance.

Other writers seek rapprochement between science and religion. For instance, John Polkinghorne, a British physicist and Anglican priest, writes prolifically as a scientist and a theologian, arguing that science and religion are complementary and can speak helpfully to each other.

How Do We Know Religious Truth?

Scripture itself testifies that God is unknowable, a mystery. We may make some inferences about God based upon the natural world, but these conclusions would not tell us whether God is gracious and loving or not.

For instance, I could infer from the orderliness of nature that God is orderly and purposeful; or I could infer from the brutality and indifference of nature that God is indifferent and cruel.

Consequently, we need God's instructions so that we can know the most important truths about God. Scripture is the primary way to know God. In the Bible, God speaks. Some Christians believe the Bible is the inerrant Word of God. Other Christians believe that the Bible is inspired (2 Timothy 3:16)—that the power of the Holy Spirit guided the biblical authors in the essential truth, if not in word-for-word dictation.

> God is a mystery to us sinful humans. Read Job 11:7-12; 37:14-18; Ecclesiastes 3:11; and Isaiah 55:8-9. Then read Romans 3:21-27 and Hebrews 1:1-3. What can we know about God, and what will always remain mysterious?

From Scripture we learn truths about the world and the universe. We learn about creation, the goal of God's plans; we learn what sin means, what salvation means; we learn about the afterlife. We learn about how God relates to the world and to human beings. We find help and consolation from ancient witnesses to the faith.

The Holy Spirit also inspires the reader. Many people read the Bible and get no truth from it. God's Spirit helps such readers recognize the truth. The Bible contains texts that are culturally conditioned, or difficult to understand and apply. The Holy Spirit guides us in this, too. Through the Spirit, God instructs us, giving us Scriptures when we most need them, clarifying passages that are unclear, and leading us to books and friends who can help us deepen our understanding.

The Spirit does not work separately from our human reason and experience. By reason we can have deeper understanding, we can cross-reference scriptural passages, we can arrive at rational insights for our lives based on scriptural truths. We also bring our

> How has the Bible helped you to know or understand God? Which Scriptures have been most meaningful to you in your journey of faith?

human experiences to bear, along with our reason. The Bible can speak to us differently at different times of our lives. This can be true of any excellent literary work, too; but in the case of the Bible, the Spirit helps us better understand the biblical texts as we grow and learn.

Prayer is crucially important in gaining religious truth. You cannot know another person without spending time with them. Even people who have been married many years discover new things about each other. In prayer, we establish and maintain a relationship with God.

My pastor, Jim McClaren, recently preached a helpful sermon about how God speaks to us. He noted that God speaks to us in a variety of circumstances: through the Bible, through other people, in dreams, in worship, through inner "promptings." God can also call us in the "desert" circumstances of our lives. But how do we know that it's God speaking and not our selfish desires or something else? The call doesn't go away, and it also brings peace. It doesn't contradict the Bible. Godly friends can affirm it for us. The call also fits our talents and abilities. Plus, when we move in that direction, resources begin to appear.

> How do you recognize God's voice? Where do you best hear, see, or experience God's truth?

Religious truth is also known through tradition. Protestant Christians stress tradition less than Roman Catholic and Orthodox Christians, but tradition nevertheless is a source of teaching for all Christians. Tradition comes from historic councils such as the Jerusalem Conference (Acts 15), which considered the use of Jewish practices within early Christianity; the Council of Nicaea in A.D. 325, which formulated the doctrine of the Trinity; and the Council of Chalcedon in A.D. 451, which formulated the doctrine of the Incarnation. Tradition also comes from great theologians. One of my own favorites, Karl Barth (1886–1968), wrote thousands of pages on theology with the stated goal of helping preachers.

Both science and religion are very human enterprises in that people don't always agree. But Jesus taught the appropriateness of solving problems together (Matthew 18:15-20). Paul, who didn't always see eye-to-eye with everyone, recognized the appropriateness of diversity as long as people share a common purpose (1 Corinthians 3:4-5).

Many Surprises Await

John Polkinghorne reminds us that science is an excellent pursuit of truth because it works. Science provides an accurate interpretation of how the world functions. Although scientific explanations do change over time, they do so because the physical world does not always conform to human expectation.[21]

God doesn't behave according to our expectations either, says Polkinghorne, and so religion and science become complementary ways of understanding the many surprises that await us as we seek to understand life and the world.[22]

Closing
Ask for God's guidance and blessing for the coming week. Offer a prayer of thanksgiving for all the ways science and religion offer help and hope in our lives. Close by singing together "How Great Thou Art."

For Further Reading
Intellectuals Don't Need God and Other Modern Myths: Building Bridges to Faith Through Apologetics, by Alister E. McGrath (Zondervan, 1993).

Quarks, Chaos, and Christianity: Questions to Science and Religion, by John Polkinghorne (Crossroad, 2005).

Religion and Science: Historical and Contemporary Issues, by Ian G. Barbour (HarperCollins, 1997).

Rocks of Ages: Science and Religion in the Fullness of Life, Stephen Jay Gould (Ballantine, 1999).

Science and Theology: An Introduction, by John Polkinghorne (Augsburg Fortress Press, 1998).

What We Believe but Cannot Prove: Today's Leading Thinkers on Science in the Age of Certainty, by John Brockman (Harper Perennial, 2006).

Notes

[1] See "E=mc^2 Explained" (Bill Willis, 1999); accesible from the Worsley School webpage at: http://www.worsleyschool.net/science/files/emc2/emc2.html.

[2] "Precession of the Perihelion of Mercury," by Dr. Jose Wudka of University of California, Riverside; available at: http://physics.ucr.edu/~wudka/Physics7/Notes_www/node98.html.

[3] These terms can be found in *The Essential Dictionary of Science*, edited by John O. E. Clark (Barnes & Noble, 2004); pages 273–74, 341–42, 577–78, 610–11, 631.

[4] "Explaining the Astronomical Appearances: How the Ptolemaic and Copernican Theories Propose to Do It," by instructor Lyman A. Baker of Kansas State University (Lyman A. Baker, 1998); available at: http://www-personal.ksu.edu/~lyman/english233/cosmos4.htm.

[5] "Diet Hype, Diet Fact," by Barbara Kantrowitz, in *Newsweek*, March 13, 2006; page 46.

[6] "DNA Study Shows Humans, Chimps Had Messy Parting," by Matt Crenson of the *Associated Press*, reported in the *Akron Beacon Journal*, May 18, 2006.

[7] *How Science Takes Stock: The Story of Meta-Analysis*, by Morton Hunt (Russell Sage Foundation, 1997); page 4.

[8] Hunt; pages 4–5.

[9] Hunt; page 5.

[10] *Religion and Science: Historical and Contemporary Issues*, by Ian G. Barbour (HarperCollins, 1997); page 35.

[11] Barbour; page 81.

[12] Barbour; page 78.

[13] Barbour; pages 79–80.

[14] "Science and Miracles," by Theodore M. Drange (Internet Infidels, Inc., 1998); available at: http://www.infidels.org/library/modern/theodore_drange/miracles.html.

[15] Barbour; page 78.

[16] Barbour; page 82.

[17] Barbour; page 81.

[18] "Science—Friend or Foe?" by Denis R. Alexander, *Cambridge Paper*, Vol. 4, No. 3, September 1995; available at: http://www.cis.org.uk/resources/articles/article_archive/-alexander_science_friendfoe.htm.

[19] *Intellectuals Don't Need God and Other Modern Myths: Building Bridges to Faith Through Apologetics*, by Alister E. McGrath (Zondervan, 1993); page 68.

[20] *Science and Religion: Are They Compatible?* edited by Paul Kurtz (Prometheus Books, 2003); page 13.

[21] *Quarks, Chaos, and Christianity: Questions to Science and Religion*, by John Polkinghorne (Crossroad, 2005); pages 7–8.

[22] Polkinghorne; page 17.

CHAPTER 3
FAITH AND REASON

Focus: This session explores ways that faith and reason are interrelated.

Gathering

Greet one another. Read aloud Romans 12:1-2. Share any prayer concerns or praises, and offer these to God along with prayers for God's presence during this session. Sing together the hymn "Take My Life, and Let It Be."

Faith Works With Reason

Oftentimes we think of religion as a matter of faith and science as a matter of reason. But as we briefly saw in the last chapter, faith does not function independently of our reason. We know certain truths by faith in the sense that our unaided reason could not help us come to those conclusions. Truths can be simple: triangles always

Read Romans 12:2-3. When Paul speaks of the renewal of the mind, is he referring to rationality or something more inclusive? Paul wrote about "the measure of faith that God has assigned" (verse 3). What do you think this means? Does God give to some people more faith than to others?

have three sides; molesting children is always wrong. But the truth can also be multifaceted: the truth of a poem is different than the truth of a scientific

We're discussing reason and faith, but do you also grow in your faith through music? Art? Literature? Physical activities? Contemplation?

Many of us fit into certain spiritual "types" where our faith is encouraged by different things. Corinne Ware in her book, *Discover Your Spiritual Type,* discusses four such types. A person with "head" spirituality likes books and ideas, while a person with "heart" spirituality likes music and spontaneous worship. A person with "mystic" spirituality appreciates intuition and nonverbal contemplation, while a person with "kingdom" spirituality appreciates goal-centered action and social justice issues. Ware notes that some people are unhappy in certain churches because the church does not fit his or her type.[1] Read Ware's book and think about what type you are.

study; and the truth of a symphony is different from the truth of a sworn testimony in court. As we seek to comprehend truth in its many aspects, reason and faith are ways of knowledge that can work together.

Faith can be non-intellectual—in the sense that our emotions, aesthetic sense, and physical activities are also related to faith. But faith should not be anti-intellectual; faith is not *against* reason.

Chuck Barnes, a retired geologist, writes,

The truths that come from prayer, from meditation, from Scripture, from faith: these are *not* entirely irrational truths. It must be *reasonable* to believe what we believe, though I would argue that to try to prove, using nothing but logic, religious truths is to engage in a meaningless exercise that misidentifies where logic works. However, still, if you insist that you believe in 'The Great Pumpkin,' then I have a responsibility to ask you how you came to that conclusion, and your explanation needs to be on your lips. If we can't explain our faith to another, I would posit that we don't have it. So the explanation and explication of one's faith are [an] inherent part of having a belief.

If someone asked you why you're a Christian, what would you say? Take some time to consider the reasons why you believe, and write those reasons down. How do you respond to Barnes' remark that we don't have faith if we can't explain it?

If we honestly can't think of ways to explain why we believe, we should not be discouraged. We may have serious doubts, we may have meager reasons for our beliefs, or we may have reasons that are so personal that they're hard to put into words. It helps to remember that God encourages even the smallest faith (Isaiah 42:3a). We should continue to explore with God the meaning of our faith, even if our journey is painful.

Biblical Ideas About Faith and Reason

How does the Bible address the subject of faith and reason?

The Bible speaks of the "heart" (in Hebrew *lēv*, in Greek *kardía*) over 900 times.[2] Although the word *kardía* has entered English as words like cardiac and cardiovascular, the Bible uses the word "heart" not simply to mean the muscle in our chest, but to describe human intellect, volition, and emotion. The heart is the seat of our reason, our will, and our affections. As Joel B. Green,

> Look up these Scriptures: Genesis 8:21; Deuteronomy 6:4-5; 10:16; Joshua 5:1; 2 Samuel 24:10; Psalm 14:1; 24:4; Jeremiah 31:33; Matthew 5:8; Luke 2:19; 1 John 3:20. What do you think the word "heart" signifies in these passages? The mind? The emotions? A combination of the two?

professor of New Testament Interpretation at Asbury Theological Seminary, told me recently, "the Hebrew Bible can refer to 'heart' without naming an organ or a metaphysically separate 'part' of the human person."

In the Bible, wisdom (Hebrew *hakkam*, Greek *sŏphia*) is not just reason but also experience combined with understanding and a moral sense. Thus the Book of Proverbs entreats us repeatedly to "find wisdom" and to "get understanding" (3:13). Wisdom never simply means acquisition of information but also moral sense and "fear of the LORD" (e.g., 1:7; 2:1-15; 3:5-8; and others).

Although Proverbs praises wisdom, other biblical authors are less "upbeat." In Job 12:7-11, Job reflects ruefully upon the omnipotence of God—though God's power is evident in nature, why has God sent him such distress? Wisdom has left him empty and confused. In Ecclesiastes, the author speaks of the discouragement of seeking wisdom: "I . . . applied my mind to seek and to search out by wisdom all that is done under heaven; it is an unhappy business that God has given to human beings to be busy with. . . . For in much wisdom is much vexation, and those who increase knowledge increase sorrow" (1:12-13, 18). Even in the Bible, wisdom only gets us so far.

Another biblical word to consider is "truth." In Hebrew the word is *'emeth*, which is related to another Hebrew word, *amen*, "so be it" or "so it is." The Greek word for truth is *alēthĕia*. In the Bible, truth is not a function of human reason—that is, the proper correspondence between statements and facts. Truth is the character of God himself, as in Hebrews 6:18: "it is impossible for God to lie" (NIV). Jesus refers to both God's Word and himself as truth (John 8:31-32; 16:13; 17:8, 17).

> How do you understand Jesus' words "I am the way, and the truth, and the life" in John 14:6? How do his words relate to Christian doctrine? How do you see the connections between Christian doctrine and the person of Jesus as presented in this Scripture?

The Bible does not make a sharp understanding among reason and emotions, volition, moral sense, common-sense wisdom, and faith. All are part of our God-created nature.

Christianity's New Orientation

Over the centuries, Christians have differed about the kinds of truths at which we arrive through faith and reason. Some Christian writers believe that faith and reason work well together; while for others, faith-knowledge is always to be preferred to reason-knowledge.

Today, science is independent of areas like theology and philosophy. In the ancient and medieval eras, however, science fit under the larger rubric of "philosophy."[3] Thus, ancient Greek philosophers also investigated the natural world. In the next several paragraphs, I use the word "philosophy" to include what we would call "the natural sciences."

Modern science owes much to the spirit of the ancient Greeks, who sought natural explanations for natural phenomena apart from religion. This is not to say the ancient Greeks were not religious. But in their curiosity and passion for truth, they sought the nature of things through close observation, investigation, and logical conclusions.

> Look up these Scriptures: Psalm 104; Proverbs 16:4a; John 1:1-3; Colossians 1:15-17; Hebrews 1:1-3. For the authors, how is God's work revealed in nature? Do we know God through faith, reason, or a combination of these?

Thales, for instance, believed that water was the most basic element in the universe. Anaximenes believed

40

the basic element was air. Others, like Democritus, believed all things were made of atoms. And other philosophers, like Empedocles and Anaxagoras, developed precursors of our modern theory of elements. These philosophers focused on the world of matter and necessity. However some Greeks worried that these philosophers undermined religion by being too rationalistic.[4]

The philosophies of Plato and Aristotle became tremendously influential for Christianity, establishing some of the basic "models" of reality. Plato (427–347 B.C.) said that theories aren't just human descriptions of things; theories are actually types of eternal truths about things. Plato called these higher truths "forms." For instance, there is a form of beauty that is eternal and unchanging, and particular beautiful things participate in this form. An individual person participates in the form of "human being." So according to Plato, human reason actually puts us in contact with eternal truths, though imperfectly.[5]

Plato's younger contemporary, Aristotle (384–322 B.C.), thought Plato's philosophy was unnecessarily complicated. The form of something, said Aristotle, is just what the thing is—not an eternal idea. Everything, he said, has substance (form) and accidents (properties).[6] My own substance is human being, and

> For centuries, Christians in the Roman Catholic tradition have believed that in the Eucharist, the bread and wine transform into the body and blood of Christ. Eventually, theologians were able to use Aristotle's philosophy to explain this long-time belief. The substance of the elements remains bread and wine but the form miraculously becomes Jesus' blood and body.[7]

my accidents are my set of characteristics or properties: I'm a middle-aged, Caucasian male with brown hair, blue eyes, and so on.

When Christianity began, it echoed some of Greek philosophy, especially Plato's. Some of Paul's letters sound platonic. When he speaks of "see[ing] through a glass, darkly" (1 Corinthians 13:12, KJV), Paul, like Plato, expresses that we have only imperfect knowledge of eternal truths—but that after death we will see things clearly. Paul also calls Jesus the "image" of the eternal God (Colossians 1:15-22; Hebrews 1:3; 8:5). Whether or not he consciously used philosophical ideas, Paul certainly used understandable images and concepts from his time period in order to communicate gospel truths. Other early Christians similarly used philosophical ideas when helpful.[8]

Something New

Christianity also contradicted some Greek ideas. For instance, for the Greeks an increase in knowledge resulted in an increase of goodness; a lack of virtue was a result of ignorance. Christians, on the other hand, maintained that knowledge could not counteract the sin within us.

For ancient Greeks, the world was seen as rational and understandable, although changing and imperfect. For Christians, the world is created by God, but it suffers because of human sin. For ancient Greeks, the process of history was dictated by fate—even the gods were subject to fate. The biblical view shows that God is involved in human history. Although we do suffer because of sin, faults in our character, and the wrongdoing of others, God is greater than all of that.[9]

Paul may have had Greek wisdom in mind when he talked about the foolishness of belief in God (1 Corinthians 1:18–2:5). The notion of a crucified Messiah makes no sense; it's oxymoronic to say that God's great leader was executed as a criminal. But we know this is true because of God's Word.

We have many wonderful gifts from the ancient Greeks—their art, architecture, and the Athenian concept of democracy. Christianity offers hope where Greek philosophy has none: a personal God who is greater than our sins and sorrows. But Christianity still uses aspects of Greek philosophy to better articulate the message of Christ.

> Preachers try to use contemporary images to communicate the gospel. References to *Star Wars* and "the Force" were popular sermon images back in the late 1970's and early 1980's. What other contemporary images—whether from popular culture, science, or other sources—could be used to communicate the gospel?

Athens and/or Jerusalem

Early Christian thinkers differed concerning the study of nature and the use of reason. Justin Martyr (ca. 100–165), Clement of Alexandria (ca. 150–215), and others praised philosophy as one way by which Christians could better understand God's truths and God's world. Origen (ca. 185–254) also praised philosophy as a method of understanding Scripture, although he cautioned that philosophers often disagreed with foundations of theology. For instance, some philosophers thought of matter as eternal.[10] Origen gave us the idea of two "books," Scripture and nature, as sources of truth about God.[11]

Not all theologians adopted philosophy. Tertullian (ca. 160–230) asked, "What . . . has Athens to do with Jerusalem?"[12] In other words, what do philosophy and science have to do with faith? Perhaps theology relies too strongly upon philosophy. Tertullian and other early theologians worried that heretics and critics of Christianity had used reason to attack sound Christian doctrine. His figurative distinction between Athens and Jerusalem has remained a metaphor contrasting reason and faith.

Augustine (354–430) was the first great theologian following Paul. Augustine was disinclined to investigate natural phenomena, or to speculate about the "natural" meanings of the world and nature. He believed that the natural world pointed to God; the glories of creation reflected the greater glory of its Creator. [13] But Augustine did appreciate philosophy and believed that reason and logic could help faith, as long as faith came first.[14] As Edward Grant, writer and professor of history and philosophy of science, notes, Augustine did not think God created the universe in six days. In the apocryphal book of Ecclesiasticus, which he considered scriptural, Augustine read that God "created all things together" (18:1). This makes rational sense, he argued, because God would not create disorderly matter first and then later give it form. Thus, using both faith and reason to arrive at his conclusions, Augustine believed that God made all things simultaneously, but for our better understanding, Genesis narrates creation in stages of six days.[15]

Many early Christian thinkers maintained that there can be only one truth, believing that faith and reason can always work together.[16]

Medieval Ideas About Faith and Reason

The Middle Ages was not a "dark age" that suppressed learning and science. For instance, people did know that the earth was round rather than flat.[17] The science then was different, however, than modern science. Philosophers viewed the world "sacramentally," that is, as a sign of invisible reality (God). As W. T. Jones puts it, this "sacramental outlook" gave people "a sense of purpose, meaningfulness, and fulfillment" that is absent in the modern outlook.[18]

Syllogistic reasoning—that is, deductive arguments that argue a specific conclusion from certain general premises—long-dominated medieval science. Unfortunately, those general premises were sometimes accepted uncritically. Thinkers instead began to use an inductive method in which specific observations of phenomena were utilized to form a hypothesis. Medieval thinkers also argued about the nature of particulars and universals. Particulars name certain things, like "Paul" and "Fluffy," while universals are the things themselves: in this case, human being and cat. Medieval philosophers believed these universals were actual things. Indeed, when we use universals like "grace" and "Trinity," they *must* be actual things because God is revealed by means of these concepts.[19]

> What is your reaction to Anselm's argument that God is "a being than which nothing greater can be conceived"? Does it make sense? Would it help people in our own time to believe in God's existence?

Anselm (ca. 1033–1109) said that faith by its very nature seeks understanding; therefore he used reason to demonstrate Christian truths. For instance, Anselm demonstrated God's existence based on logical reasoning. Anselm said that God is "a being than which nothing greater can be conceived." That is, if we have an idea of a perfect being (God), then that perfect being must necessarily exist because, otherwise, our idea of God is imperfect.[20]

Peter Abelard (1079–1142) taught that faith should be rigorously examined by reason and evidence in order to discover inconsistencies and errors. Some of his contemporaries believed he thereby undermined Christian faith and confused new Christians.[21] But his method remained and influenced Thomas Aquinas (ca. 1225–1274), one of the greatest Christian theologians. Aquinas affirmed sciences as sources of proper knowledge. Reason unaided by faith can even help demonstrate the

> Thomas Aquinas argued that we can demonstrate God's existence in five ways:
>
> 1) Things are in motion, but what caused motion in the first place? We understand that "first mover" to be God. 2) We understand cause-effect relationships, but what was the first cause? We call the first cause God. 3) Things move from possibility to necessity, and God began all future necessities. 4) Things in the universe are in orders of greater and lesser complexity. God is the author of both simple and complex forms. 5) Things in the universe are orderly and governed, and we call God the source of order and governance.[22]
>
> Can you think of any similar relationships in the universe that fit Aquinas' demonstrations?

existence of God. But for Aquinas, science and reason only give us so much knowledge; we also need revealed truth and faith in order to have right knowledge of God. Reason alone can't give us Christ.

Renaissance and Reformation

During the fourteenth century, Renaissance scholars were interested in textual criticism. They examined documents and manuscripts from earlier times, discovered copying errors, compared versions, and studied texts as a scientist would examine a natural object. Although many of these scholars were religious, they unintentionally elevated reason to an equal, and even higher, role as revelation: If an individual investigator can discover truths without recourse to the church, perhaps anyone can discover truths without the authority of the church.[23]

In discovering ancient Greek texts, Renaissance scholars regained the Greek interest in drawing truth from the empirical observation of nature. Universities, which had been growing in Europe since the thirteenth century, supported free scientific inquiry.[24] Several factors like these helped spur the momentum of science.

The advancement of science did not begin as a rebellion against religion, but as an implicit rebellion against the authority of the Roman Catholic Church. Martin Luther (1483–1546) was not a scientist; but he argued that anyone could read and understand the Bible without the help of the Pope. Luther thought that reason could *potentially* lead a person astray. Reason, for instance, tells us we have to please God by our own efforts; it doesn't make rational sense to think the Holy God loves sinners.[25]

Luther's innovation, combined with the Renaissance interest in science and textual examination, helped set the stage for the rise of scientific method. Along with other economic and social aspects of European history at the time, the authority of the institutional Church was weakening, which allowed a new kind of freedom of inquiry that was independent of any theological authorities—whether the Pope, the church fathers, or ultimately the Bible.[26] (The case of Galileo, which I discuss in Chapter 5, partly reflects the difficult situation of Roman Catholic Church during that time.)

As J.C.C. Smart also puts it,

> It could very plausibly be argued that Christian theology was an important condition of the development of modern science, since the idea of God as

ruler of the universe made men sympathetic to the idea that God had arranged things in an orderly way and that there were laws of nature which could be discovered if one tried hard enough.[27]

Rise of Science

The 1600's and 1700's are described as the Age of Reason, or the Enlightenment. Altogether, it was an optimistic age. Newly-discovered scientific laws showed that the universe is orderly and predictable. Some scientists were very friendly toward religion, including Gassendi, Boyle, Newton, Descartes, and many others. But confidence in science also led to questions about religion. For some writers of the time, religion offered unprovable doctrinal claims; but through reliance upon facts and reason, science could free people from superstition. Indeed, God created the universe in such an amazing, orderly way, though God needn't necessarily continue to be part of the functioning of the natural world.[28]

Several historical trends and events dashed the optimism. One such event was the French Revolution, which, far from bringing reason and freedom, deteriorated into violence and terror. The Industrial Revolution also hurt optimism in human potential; technology made worse rather than better the lives of many workers.

Another influential philosopher was René Descartes (1596–1650). Descartes uttered the famous phrase, "I think, therefore I am" (Latin, *cogito ergo sum*). Descartes said that we can potentially doubt everything—except the fact that we are thinking. Therefore, we cannot doubt our own existence. Consequently, we cannot doubt God's existence, because God would not allow us to be deceived about our own existence. Critics say that Descartes, like Anselm, provided a circular kind of proof of God. Others complain that Descartes made a problematic split between reason and reality—that is, between mind and matter.[29]

> What feelings or thoughts do you have about Descartes' famous phrase, "I think, therefore I am"?

One major thinker of the Enlightenment era was Immanuel Kant (1724–1804). Seeking to safeguard the proper boundaries of faith and reason, Kant maintained that we perceive and understand reality according to the forms and categories of the mind. We do not know reality as it is in itself, apart from our perception. But we all have a common mental "apparatus" by which we ascertain and understand the world. Thus, since God is not perceived in the same way as the world, Kant said that we cannot know God by "pure" reason. But we can know God through "practical" reason, the inner moral law that is operative as we make choices. [30]

> How do you respond to Kant's idea that we know God through "practical reason"?

Kant's philosophy is still quite strongly felt today. By separating rational knowledge from faith knowledge, Kant (along with other Enlightenment forces and the earlier Martin Luther) helped introduce an enduring individualism to religion.[31] How do we know if religion is true? My own inner sense of the moral law gives me a sense of God. Religious belief, therefore, becomes a comparatively private thing, even though it has definite social and public effects.

> In what sense is religious belief a private or individual matter? In what sense is it social and public?

In our modern time, it's difficult to envision religion without an Enlightenment sense of individualism. One of the approaches of this book, in fact, is to help you reflect upon your own personal experience of religious faith.

In more recent times, two authors have maintained that science and religion are not in harmony. In 1874, John William Draper (1811–1882) wrote *History of the Conflict Between Religion and Science*. Several years later, in 1896, Andrew Dickson White (1832–1918) published a long work called *A History of the Warfare of Science With Theology in Christendom*. In it, White compares human progress to a river and Christian theology to ice that clogs the river. However, White was more positive toward religion than the earlier Draper, who was strongly anti-Catholic.[32] While historians have questioned

> Do you agree or disagree with the view that science and religion are not in harmony? Why?

some of their judgments, the works of Draper and White created a lasting impression, still influential in our own time—that religion and science are necessarily in conflict, with progressive science hindered by regressive theology.[33]

Our World

Many people have the impression that science is an imperious, secular movement that threatens religious truth. But as we've seen in this very brief overview, Christianity itself helped give rise to science, not only during the last five hundred years, but also in Christianity's traditional, congenial approach to reason as a complement to faith.

How might Christians communicate the gospel in our scientific world? What do we have that's new and hopeful? How can Christians respect the wisdom of modern science while also proving the truth of the gospel? How might Christians join traditional faith and contemporary reason in our own time?

David Wilkinson of St. Johns College, University of Durham, writes that "Christians need to stand against the tide of the current trend of science bashing. The birth of modern science came from the Christian conviction that science was a gift from God for exploring the world and in bringing healing to creation. Responsibility was given to use this gift wisely. . . . We need to recapture that sense of gift and responsibility."[34]

In the following three chapters, we will look at a few specific, scientific topics that speak to our religious convictions.

Closing
Close by reading in unison Deuteronomy 6:4-5.

For Further Reading
Reconstructing Nature: The Engagement of Science and Religion, by John Brooke and Geoffrey Cantor (Oxford University Press, 2000).

Religion and Science: Historical and Contemporary Issues, by Ian G. Barbour (HarperCollins, 1997).

Science and Religion, 1450–1900: From Copernicus to Darwin, by Richard G. Olson, (Greenwood Press, 2004).

Science and Religion, 400 B.C. to A.D. 1550: From Aristotle to Copernicus, by Edward Grant (Greenwood Press, 2004).

Science and Religion: A Historical Introduction, edited by Gary B. Ferngren (Johns Hopkins University Press, 2002).

Notes

[1] *Discover Your Spiritual Type: A Guide to Individual and Congregational Growth*, by Corinne Ware (The Alban Institute, Inc., 1995); pages 36–45, 84–85.

[2] *The Zondervan Pictorial Bible Dictionary*, edited by Merrill C. Tenney (Zondervan, 1967); page 340.

[3] *Science and Religion, 400 B.C. to A.D. 1550: From Aristotle to Copernicus*, by Edward Grant (Greenwood Press, 2004); page 103.

[4] Grant; pages 57–60.

[5] "Greek Philosophy: Plato," from the website of Washington State University (Richard Hooker, 1996); available at: http://www.wsu.edu/~dee/GREECE/PLATO.HTM.

[6] See "Aristotle on Substance and Accident," on the University of Leeds website; accessible at: http://www.philosophy.leeds.ac.uk/GMR/hmp/modules/ihmp0304/units/unit07/aristotle.html.

[7] See "The Real Presence of Christ in the Eucharist," from "New Advent" web resource base (Kevin Knight, 2006); available at: http://www.newadvent.org/cathen/05573a.htm.

[8] Grant; page 105.

[9] "The Greek Versus the Hebrew View of Man," excerpted from George Eldon Ladd's *The Pattern of New Testament Truth*, in *Present Truth Magazine*, Vol. 29, Article 2; accessible at: http://www.presenttruthmag.com/archive/XXIX/29-2.htm.

[10] Grant; pages 106–09.

[11] *Science and Religion, 1450–1900: From Copernicus to Darwin*, by Richard G. Olson (Greenwood Press, 2004); page 2.

[12] "Tertullian of Carthage, Early Church Father" (Phoenicia.org, 2006); available at: http://phoenicia.org/tertullian2.html.

[13] *A History of Western Philosophy: The Medieval Mind*, second edition, by W. T. Jones (Harcourt Brace Jovanovich, 1969); pages 131–33.

[14] Grant; pages 111–14.

[15] Grant; page 131–32.

[16] Grant; pages 13–14.

[17] Grant; page 5.

[18] Jones, *The Medieval Mind*; page xix.

[19] Jones, *The Medieval Mind*; pages 185–90.

[20] Jones, *The Medieval Mind*; pages 201–03.

[21] Jones, *The Medieval Mind*; pages 190–201.

[22] *The Summa Theologica of Saint Thomas Aquinas*, translated by Fathers of the English Dominican Province (Encyclopædia Brittanica, Inc., 1952); pages 12–13.

[23] *A History of Western Philosophy: Hobbes to Hume*, by W. T. Jones, second edition (Harcourt, Brace & World, Inc., 1969); pages 36–38.

[24] Grant; pages 247–48.

[25] *The Theology of Martin Luther*, by Paul Althaus, translated by Robert C. Schultz (Fortress Press, 1966); page 123.

[26] Jones, *Hobbes to Hume*; pages 57, 64–66.

[27] *The Encyclopedia of Philosophy*, Vol. 7, edited by Paul Edwards (Macmillan Publishing Co., Inc. & The Free Press, 1967); page 159. Note, however, that Smart is not thereby defending the truth of religion in this passage.

[28] *A History of Western Philosophy: Kant and the Nineteenth Century*, revised second edition, by W. T. Jones (Harcourt Brace Jovanovich, 1975); pages 1–8. See also *Science and Religion: A Historical Introduction*, edited by Gary B. Ferngren (Johns Hopkins University Press, 2002); pages 143–52.

[29] Jones, *Hobbes to Hume*; pages 164–68.

[30] Jones, *Kant and the Nineteenth Century*; pages 53–57, 66–68.

[31] Olson; pages 1–2.

[32] *Rocks of Ages: Science and Religion in the Fullness of Life*, by Stephen Jay Gould (Ballantine, 1999); pages 99–103.

[33] Ferngren; pages ix–x.

[34] From "The Christian Value of Science," by Dr. David Wilkinson, in the *Methodist Recorder*, November 1999.

CHAPTER 4
CREATION AND EVOLUTION

Focus: This chapter examines the basics of evolutionary theory and the argument of intelligent design.

Gathering
Greet one another and share highlights of your lives since you last met. Brainstorm all the things you can think of concerning evolution. What is the extent of your present understanding of the theory? Pray for God's presence and guidance as you study this session together. Sing together the hymn "All Things Bright and Beautiful."

Did You Peek?

Some of you may have leafed over to this chapter first! Evolution is by far the most controversial aspect of the science-religion debate. Even the term "Darwinism," a misnomer, implies that the theory isn't a science but an ideology, like Marxism or Leninism. Proponents and opponents alike are likely to become very passionate about their views on evolution.

Can you believe in evolution and still be religious? My answer is yes, but in this

> How do you respond to the question, "Can you believe in evolution and still be religious?"

chapter, I want to lay out several of the issues in a straightforward manner. In a study such as this one, I cannot give a comprehensive treatment of a topic that has generated thousands of books, articles, and news stories. Let my thoughts be the beginning of your further study.

Darwin's Discovery

The British scientist Charles Darwin (1809–1882) didn't "invent" the theory of evolution. Ancient Greek philosophers speculated that humans developed from animal ancestors. Scientists prior to Darwin's time offered theories that set the stage for his studies.[1]

The Swedish biologist Carolus Linnaeus (1707–1778) classified animals and plants according to types. Linnaeus believed these types were divinely created but recognized variations within types and similarities among animals (humans and apes, for instance). For him, animals, plants, and inanimate objects made up a "chain of being."[2]

The French scientist Jean Baptist Lamarck (1774–1829) first offered a theory of evolution. He believed in the "chain of being," but he also believed that animals developed certain traits in response to particular challenges—as certain organs grew stronger and others weaker, these traits passed to offspring. A giraffe's long neck is an example.[3]

Other scientists and writers influenced Darwin. Thomas Malthus (1766–1834) wrote about population increase and food supply.[4] Charles Lyell (1797–1875) theorized that the earth's geological evidence suggests millions of years of development, rather than a few thousand years.[5]

Research about the geology and geography of the earth also appeared during the 1800's. Uniformitarianism derives from the work of the Scottish geologist James Hutton in the late 1700's. The term was first used by a Cambridge scientist, William Whewell, in 1832. According to the theory, the earth's geology and geography came into being by natural processes active over a very long time. Sir Charles Lyell's scientific work, published in the 1830's, confirmed the theory.[6] Chuck Barnes, a retired geologist, writes, "Uniformitarianism asserts that the processes operating on Earth today are similar to those that operated billions of years ago. Therefore, we can interpret the ancient *products* of these processes correctly in geologic history."

Archbishop James Ussher was a seventeenth-century Anglican who used the biblical genealogies and his own assumptions and surmises to date Creation as happening in 4004 B.C. His dating system gained widespread acceptance in church circles because it was included in editions of the King James Bible.[7] Uniformitarianism was controversial because it contradicted the more biblically-consistent theory, catastrophism, which postulated that the earth was supernaturally created and later altered through catastrophes like the Flood.[8]

My Bible dictionary's entry on Genesis gives reasons for an evangelical rejection of uniformitarianism: 1) the Hebrew words in Genesis 1 for "evening and morning" indicate 24 hours rather than great eons of time; 2) a universal flood would have created tremendous geological change, and so catastrophism is a suitable model; and 3) Adam was given authority over all the animals, and the text never mentions earlier, extinct species.[9]

> Look up "creation" in several Bible dictionaries. How does your research inform or challenge your views? Explain.

Darwin provided scientific evidence for evolutionary theory. In his early career Darwin studied medicine briefly, became interested in biology, and also earned a degree in theology from Cambridge. In 1831, when he was 22, Darwin joined a mapping expedition, which lasted five years. On that journey aboard the H.M.S. *Beagle*, Darwin studied Charles Lyell's research into the earth's great geological age.

When the expedition reached the Galápagos Islands, 600 miles from the coast of South America in the Pacific, Darwin observed that the species of finches on the islands looked different from the single species on the South American coast. Furthermore, the finches exhibited different beak varieties depending on which island they lived. Some of the birds developed beaks that could crush seeds in areas where seeds were hard, while other birds developed more prominent beaks that could catch insects, and so on.

Darwin theorized that these variations occurred over generations in order for the birds to adapt to different diets on different islands. In turn, birds with better beaks for certain environments mated, and their species tended to be favored over time. This phenomenon was called natural selection.[10]

A Well-Timed Idea

When Darwin returned home in 1836, he did not immediately publish his findings because of the complex religious and political situation in England at that time. When he did publish *On the Origin of Species* in

1859, the first edition sold out the first day.[11] Later, in 1871, Darwin published *The Descent of Man*, wherein he argued that that creatures select the best mates, and thus desirable traits are preserved through succeeding generations. These two books established Darwin's theories. Another naturalist named Alfred Wallace (1823–1913) developed a very similar theory of natural selection. Wallace's research was conducted later than Darwin's but the two men published their findings at about the same time.[12]

Neither Darwin nor Wallace knew of the research of Gregor Mendel (1822–1884), a Catholic priest who developed theories of genetics based on his experiments on breeding pea plants. He realized that traits of living things are contained in pairs of units (genes), which divide when cells split. Mendel's research provided insight into something that Darwin himself did not grasp: how traits of two parents are passed on from one generation to another.[13]

What is your response to the scientific views mentioned? Do you think such views contradict religious views? Why or why not?

Another scientist, Hugo De Vries (1848–1935) observed how mutations and variants in primroses tended to pass along their variations to subsequent generations. Unlike Darwin, he believed that evolution occurs in "leaps" rather than by very gradual change, a position held by several subsequent theorists.[14] Yet another scientist, Jacques Boucher Crèvecœur de Perthes (1788–1868), published his theories on prehistoric artifacts which, he said, must have been made by earlier types of human beings. His theories had just gained scientific acceptance at the time of Darwin's first publication.[15]

Closer to our own time, scientists in the 1940's wedded genetics to evolutionary theory ("neo-Darwinism"), greatly clarifying the process of species development. Recent research has focused on the development of animals from embryos into adults (evolution and development, or "Evo Devo").[16]

What Is Evolutionary Theory?

When critics say that "evolution is just a theory," they misuse the word theory. Evolution is not a hypothesis, like the debate about whether eggs are bad for your arteries. Although scientists continue to debate aspects of evolution, it is recognized as a satisfactory theory within the scientific community. It meets the criteria we saw in Chapter 2: it provides a framework for understanding natural phenomena, it holds as a theory as ongoing experiments are conducted, and it provides an excellent framework in multiple areas of inquiry—paleontology, biology, genetics, and geology.

> What comes to your mind when you hear the word "theory"? How does the explanation of theory as a framework for understanding natural phenomena inform your understanding of the world?

Chuck Barnes points out that in reproduction, genes are passed along from one generation to the next. But genes also respond to environmental challenges so that, across several generations, species develop qualities that allow it to survive. Genes change (in a process called mutation or, more currently, "genetic drift"); new characteristics and new species emerge. Thus animals have, within their genes, a natural process that helps encourage long-term success in an environment. Even with this process, success is not ensured. Scientists tell us that over 99% of all species that have lived on earth have become extinct.

Dinosaur fossils have been known for centuries, but the creatures have only been scientifically described since the early nineteenth century. During the mid-1800's, dinosaurs were designated as species of reptiles and, although not lizards, were given name from two Greek words meaning "fearfully-great" and "lizard."[17]

Chuck Barnes notes that when sea turtles are born, 92% of the newborns are eaten by birds before they can reach the sea. Those 8% that survive have strong legs/flippers that allow them to make it to the sea. They can run faster. The genes that dictate strong legs will be passed down to the next generation. He cites another example of evolution. Fossil evidence shows us that, millions of years ago, one species of squirrel existed in all of northern Arizona. But as the Colorado Plateau rose and the Grand Canyon began to form, squirrels at the North Rim of the Grand Canyon, cut off from the warmer climates to the south, developed more fur and bushier tails. They adapted to the colder climate. Indeed, the Kaibab squirrels, as they are called, are found nowhere else in the world but the North Rim region. Meanwhile, squirrels south of the canyon (called Abert's squirrels) adapted to the more moderate climate and are more prevalent in the Southwest. Because of long-term environmental changes, the genes of the squirrels changed and were passed on, resulting in two species.

Evolution is observable today. Have you ever been scolded by a doctor or nurse, as I have, for not taking all of your antibiotics? Bacteria can develop resistance to antibiotics. Chuck Barnes points out that "tuberculosis, one of the most dangerous diseases to humankind, is becoming a modern example of evolution. The 'fittest' tubercular bacteria under antibiotic pressure have survived, their adaptation has been encoded in their DNA, and resistant individuals have prospered to establish a new drug-resistant species."

As Chuck Barnes puts it, evolution is both an observational and an inferential truth. It is an observational truth because we can observe species changes in both animals and bacteria; the theory is a reasonable explanation for these phenomena of change. Evolution is also an inferential truth because we can compare, for instance, body types and genetic makeup and infer certain connections among species. We can compare characteristics among members of our own families, of course; but we can also compare similarities between human beings and animals like chimpanzees, with which we share a 98% DNA similarity.

"Both observational and inferential truths," he says, "point toward evolution as a highly probable fact. The theory to explain those facts can be challenged, and it typically is challenged—daily—primarily by bioscientists, as they continue to try to improve its reliability and predictability. But it—the theory—successfully predicts both our past and the future of life."

Evolution in the News

Read the judge's decision in the Dover, PA, school board case, which many supporters have applauded as an excellent statement concerning the teaching of evolution in public schools (http://www.pamd.uscourts.gov/kitzmiller/kitzmiller_342.pdf). It's a long decision but worthwhile to read. What are the judge's key points? Why does he think intelligent design is not suitable to be taught as science? Do you agree or disagree? Why?

Evolution has been an issue in recent years. State and local school board members in several states have variously tried to attach disclaimers to textbooks concerning evolution, and even to introduce science lesson plans that include intelligent design. These measures have not been successful; in fact, a federal judge declared the teaching of intelligent design as unconstitutional.

Many Americans are ambivalent about evolution in spite of its long-time high standing in the scientific community. According to a Pew Research Center survey, 64% of Americans are open to the teaching of both creationism and evolution in public schools.[18] Part of that ambivalence stems from erroneous notions. For instance, humans are not evolved from modern apes and monkeys. According to evolutionary theory, humans and primates descended from common ancient ancestors. Scientists believe that humans evolved from the species *Australopithecus anamensis*, which lived about four million years ago. This species evolved when certain apes moved from the forests into the savannahs and eventually, out of necessity, walked upright. Other species of *Australopithecus* evolved, including *Australopithecus afranensis* and *Australopithecus africanus*. But over two million years ago, *Homo habilis* evolved, and eventually *Homo erectus*, which lived not only in Africa but Eurasia as well. *Homo sapiens* and the similar species *Homo neanderthalensis* evolved differently from *Homo habilis*, although scientists are currently still debating the various connections from the fossil evidence. Recently, fossils of a possibly different species, the small *Homo floresiensis*, were discovered near Java.[19] *National Geographic* recently reported that scientists are now using DNA evidence, in addition to fossils, to trace the development of ancient human species.[20]

Another misconception concerning evolutionary theory is that it contains "holes" and discrepancies; and therefore public school students should know about alternative theories. Actually, as I wrote earlier, evolutionary theory is the basis of several modern sciences—no substantial controversy about the theory exists among scientists. The "holes" and "gaps" are areas of ongoing discovery, which is true in all scientific theories.

> Read Genesis 1 and 2. What do these chapters say to you about God? About human beings? How do these narratives relate to or inform your faith? How do your readings of these Scriptures connect to the scientific discoveries about common ancestors for modern apes and humans?

Scientists disagree that creationism and intelligent design really are alternative theories because they do not fit the criteria of scientific theories: they are not provable through experiments, nor debated or tested through the processes of peer review and ongoing testing. Scientists complain that pro-creation adherents distort the facts, most notably the idea that we should teach "'both sides of the argument.'" According to scientists, the real argument is waged by non-scientists who attack the theory through faulty understanding, appeals to emotion, or other unsuitable means.[21]

Evolutionary theory worries many religious people for interrelated reasons. The theory contradicts a literal reading of Genesis, which of course states that the world was created in six days about 6,000 years ago ("young earth" creationism insists on conformity of science to Genesis 1). The evolutionary theory also seems to eliminate the necessity of God's "providence," that is, God's governance and care for creation. Perhaps most seriously, evolution seems to lessen the seriousness of sin and grace. If human beings developed cognition and volition through a genetic, evolutionary process, then human sin is an outcome of our species development, too. Would God become human if sin were merely the result of our genetic development?[22]

> Many Scriptures testify to God's creation and governance of the world. Break into groups and study some or all of these Scriptures: Deuteronomy 10:14-15; 1 Chronicles 29:11-12; Job 9:5-10; Psalm 89:11; 95:3-5; 135:6; Proverbs 19:21; Ecclesiastes 3:14; Isaiah 45:11-12; Daniel 4:34-35; Ephesians 1:9-11; Colossians 1:15-17; Hebrews 2:8b-9; Revelation 20:11-13. Discuss how these passages variously speak to our topic.

Criticisms of the Theory

Although scientists have reasonable refutations and explanations, evolutionary theory has been subject to criticism. One criticism is that Darwin relied too simplistically on homology (that is, traits shared by different species) in order to claim common descent. Do similar features among species necessarily imply shared ancestry?[23] Scientists would say yes.

Some people maintain that the second law of thermodynamics disproves evolution. This law states that matter and energy tend to spread out rather than cohere; for instance, water evaporates. Thus, according to this law, simple species would not evolve into complex ones. But this law does not mean that *all* matter breaks down into simpler forms (for instance, water, salt, sugar, and many other compounds do not routinely break down into their constitutive elements). Simple forms do cohere into more complex forms.[24]

Others complain that that evolution encourages a "survival of the fittest" philosophy. True, evolutionary theory has been used to promote political doctrines. But it is misused that way; evolutionary theory has to do with scientific observation of natural phenomena, not with politics, sociology, or economics.

Others complain that evolution is based on a tautology, that is, a redundancy: species survive because they are fit to survive; and they are fit to survive because they do survive. The theory of evolution thus gives no real reason why species do survive.[25] Scientists note that natural selection is a process rather than a mysterious, impersonal "cause" of survival, although our use of the term misleadingly implies that selection and evolution are causal forces.[26]

Still others wonder how genetic drift alone can result in the variety of species and the complex mechanisms of nature, especially if one accepts the premise that all species have developed from very simple, ancient organisms. Evolution supporters note that species development can certainly take shape over millions of years, but intelligent design supporters differ.

Intelligent Design

Intelligent design (ID) tries to steer between an uncritical acceptance of evolution and a literal reading of Genesis. In ID theory, certain natural phenomena are considered too complex to be attributed to natural selection and genetic drift, even over millions of years. An example comes from a precursor theory by the early nineteenth-century author William Paley, who said that if we examine a watch, we assume that someone with great skill designed the watch. If one found such a watch in the grass, one could not assume that natural forces alone brought it into being. Thus, we can infer the existence of a "designer" who created the complexity that we observe in nature.[27]

> Many people love the writings of Annie Dillard. Some of her books, notably *Pilgrim at Tinker Creek* (Harper Magazine Press, 1974) and *Teaching a Stone to Talk* (Harper & Row, 1982), express wonder at the natural world. She looks at the extravagant, fecund, and often cruel and horrible aspects of nature and raises the question, What kind of God creates like this? What about the natural world challenges you or makes you curious about the nature of God?

The ID movement started in the United States in the 1990's[28] as an alternative to evolution but is a different argument than traditional natural theology like Paley's. ID centers on an observable phenomenon: complexity in nature. Think of the DNA molecule, or the "bacterial flagellum," which is a kind of motor that propels certain bacteria. This flagellum has intricate and efficient mechanisms, yet it is microscopic in size. Think of complicated natural mechanisms like the eye, or the clotting process of the blood. Could complex forms such as these have arisen over time strictly by genetic chance? Logically, the answer seems to be no.

This is the argument for "irreducible complexity." Some natural phenomena result from natural causes; ID supporters accept many aspects of evolutionary theory. They are not creationists who believe that God created the universe in literal 24-hour days a few thousand years ago. But ID supporters argue that natural selection alone cannot account for many complex forms in nature. ID proponents seek to identify natural and intelligent causes within natural phenomena.

William Dembski, a mathematician and philosopher, has written several books on ID. He maintains that ID is a more scientific way of accounting for the natural process because it removes something false and foreign from scientific theory; that is, it is a materialistic philosophy.[29] Although science still cannot make theological statements—for instance, who the creator and designer of the universe is—ID allows for a helpful connection between science and religion.

Criticism of ID

Critics maintain that ID is not a scientific theory but rather a religious doctrine or philosophy that relies upon science and logic. Since science looks for "natural" explanations for natural phenomena, it is unscientific to infer a designer from nature's complexity—a designer that cannot be subject to observation, data, calculations, and other hallmarks of good science. ID supporters would counter that it is actually unscientific to infer blind chance to the development of complex biological forms.[30]

> What is your response to the views of intelligent design?

Another criticism is that ID can say nothing about the identity of the designer. The designer could be God, or several gods, or extraterrestrial aliens, or something else. ID supporters would counter that no science, including ID, proposes theological explanations; but ID can open possible avenues of dialogue between religion and science.[31]

Some critics of ID argue from religious grounds. Editor of the journal *Science and Christian Belief*, Denis Alexander of St. Edmund's College, Cambridge, notes that although the word "design" is not a biblical term applied to God, certain Scriptures certainly praise the natural order as the result of God's word—for instance Psalm 19 and Romans 1.[32] But he also argues that God is the author and sustainer of the whole of nature, not just the very complex aspects. Alexander fears that ID makes theologically-untenable distinctions between phenomena arising through natural selection and those specifically designed by God.[33] Again, ID supporters argue that they're doing science, not theology.

God's Governance

Evolutionary theory seems threatening because it, among other scientific theories, seems especially prone to metaphysical reductionism. One scientist, Richard Dawkins, even declared that evolution allowed him to be an "intellectually fulfilled atheist."[34] On the other hand, Kenneth R. Miller, in his book *Finding Darwin's God*, writes, "For far too long, the critics of religion have used Genesis as a convenient punching bag." Even St. Augustine, Miller notes, discouraged a "scientific" reading of Genesis, lest scoffers "show up vast ignorance in a Christian and laugh it to scorn." The truth of Genesis, said Augustine, is spiritual but no less true thereby.[35]

The apologetics website, "Answers in Genesis," criticizes evolutionary and "old earth" theories and provides several articles and topics: www.answersingenesis.org. Read some of these. How do you respond to the ideas?

Evolutionary theory is not going to go away anytime soon. So how should Christians react to evolution? One way is to criticize the theory, but do so honestly with a grasp of scientific arguments about the theory. Do not be content to say, "Evolution contradicts the Book of Genesis."

Some denominations are helping people understand creation-evolution debates. For instance, the Episcopal Church has published a "Catechism of Creation" that encourages dialogue between religion and science. It can be found at: http://www.episcopalchurch.org/science. Read the information. How do you respond?

Another way Christians can react to evolutionary theory is to uphold evolution as a legitimate theory that does, indeed, enjoy widespread consensus in the scientific community, while warning against a false philosophy, such as metaphysical reductionism. This way, we distinguish between the proper science and the philosophical conclusions that one may draw from science.

Another reaction is to uphold evolution as simply the way God has set up the world (or to put it more accurately, evolution is the most consistent scientific theory available today that can explain the way God has set up the world). Even Scripture attests to the struggle for survival in the natural world (Psalm 104:21; Job 38:41; 39:1-4, 14-16, 27-30).

> Read Psalm 104:21; Job 38:41; 39:1-4, 14-16, 27-30. What connections do you see to the struggle for survival in the natural world?

Still another way is not to dismiss evolution, but to ask the question, "How do we know God primarily?" Is it through the natural process? Through a scientific theory? Or because of God's acts in history and God's son, Jesus Christ? This is not an anti-science assertion, but it upholds the primacy of God's revelation in Jesus Christ as the way by which we know God.

> An article on "providence" in the *Baker Theological Dictionary of the Bible* states, "Although the plan of God has been partially revealed to us, in its totality it remains an ultimate mystery. We are not capable of grasping what it ultimately means because God himself is ultimately beyond us (Job 11:7-9; 26:14; 36:26; Ecclesiastes 3:11; 11:5; Isaiah 40:28; 55:8). This limitation on our part is not designed by God to humiliate us, but to humble us, to help us realize our creaturely status and find our appropriate place in his scheme of things."[36] How do you respond to these thoughts?

One of my favorite Bible verses is a truth that I know by faith, but cannot prove by science: "Are not two sparrows sold for a penny? Yet not one of them will fall to the ground apart from your Father" (Matthew 10:29). When we reflect upon the processes of nature, we marvel all the more at both the infinity and specificity of God's tender care, as well as the intricacies and mysteries of life itself.

Closing

As a class project, memorize Matthew 10:29-31, a source of wonderful comfort in times of trouble. Close by thanking God for the things you've learned so far in these lessons. Ask God to guide and protect you during the coming week.

For Further Reading

For a pro-intelligent design perspective, see *Darwin's Black Box: The Biochemical Challenge to Evolution*, by Michael J. Behe (Free Press, 2006).

For a pro-evolution perspective, see *Darwin's Dangerous Idea: Evolution and the Meanings of Life*, by Daniel C. Dennett (Simon and Schuster, 1996).

For a pro-intelligent design perspective, see *The Design Revolution: Answering the Toughest Questions About Intelligent Design*, by William A. Dembski (InterVarsity Press, 2004).

Finding Darwin's God: A Scientist's Search for Common Ground Between God and Evolution, by Kenneth R. Miller (Harper Perennial, 2000).

From So Simple a Beginning: Darwin's Four Great Books (Voyage of the Beagle, The Origin of Species, The Descent of Man, The Expression of Emotions in Man and Animals), by Charles Darwin, edited by Edward O. Wilson (W. W. Norton, 2005).

The Language of God: A Scientist Presents Evidence for Belief, by Francis S. Collins (Free Press, 2006).

For a critical look at evolution, see *The Politically Incorrect Guide™ to Science*, by Tom Bethell (Regnery Publishing, Inc., 2005).

For an explanation of evolutionary theory, see *Smithsonian Intimate Guide to Human Origins*, by Carl Zimmer (Madison Press Books, 2005).

Notes

[1] *Encyclopedia Americana, International Edition*, Vol. 10 (Scholastic Library Publishing, Inc., 2005); page 734.

[2] *Encyclopedia Americana*, Vol. 10; page 734.

[3] *Encyclopedia Americana*, Vol. 10; page 735.

[4] See "Darwin and Natural Selection," from "Early Theories of Evolution," a website created by Dr. Dennis O'Neil of Palomar College (Dennis O'Neil, 1997–2006); accessible at: http://anthro.palomar.edu/evolve/evolve_2.htm.

[5] See "Chapter 10: Introduction to the Lithosphere," from the online textbook, *Fundamentals of Physical Geography*, second edition, by Dr. Michael Pidwirny, University of British Columbia Okanagan (Michael Pidwirny, 1999–2006); accessible from: http://www.physicalgeography.net/fundamentals/10c.html.

[6] See note 5 above.

[7] From the Christian History Institute website (Christian History Institute, 1999–2006); available at: http://chi.gospelcom.net/DAILYF/2003/10/daily-10-23-2003.shtml.

[8] See note 5 above.

[9] *The Zondervan Pictorial Bible Dictionary*, edited by Merrill C. Tenney (Zondervan, 1967); pages 305–06.

[10] See note 4 above.

[11] See note 4 above.

[12] *Encyclopedia Americana*, Vol. 10; page 736.

[13] *Encyclopedia Americana*, Vol. 10; page 736–37. Also, see note 4 above.

[14] *Encyclopedia Americana*, Vol. 10; page 739.

[15] See note 4 above.

[16] See "Evolving Evolution," by Edward Ziff and Israel Rosenfeld, in *The New York Review of Books*, Vol. 53, No. 8, May 11, 2006; accessible at: http://www.nybooks.com/-articles/18970.

[17] See "Early Dinosaur Discoveries in North America," from the website of the Univsersity of California Museum of Paleontology (Regents of the University of California, 1994–2006); available at: http://www.ucmp.berkeley.edu/diapsids/dinodiscoveriesna.html. See also "Top 10 Misconceptions About Dinosaurs," compiled by M.K. Brett-Surman, Donald F. Glut, and Thomas R. Holtz, from the website of the National Museum of Natural History, Smithsonian Institute; available at: http://www.nmnh.si.edu/paleo/faq.html.

[18] See the Pew report, "Public Divided on Origins of Life: Religion a Strength and Weakness for Both Parties," posted August 30, 2005 (Pew Forum on Religion and Public Life, 2000–06); available at: http://pewforum.org/surveys/origins/.

[19] "The Proper Study of Mankind," *The Economist*, December 24, 2005, pages 6–7.

[20] "The Greatest Journey," by James Shreeve, in *National Geographic*, Vol. 209, No. 3, March 2006; pages 61–69.

[21] "Introduction to Evolutionary Biology," by Chris Colby (Talk.Origins Archive, 2006); accessible at: http://www.talkorigins.org/faqs/faq-intro-to-biology.html. See specifically the section entitled, "Scientific Standing of Evolution and Its Critics." This is a good article that discusses current thinking on evolutionary theory.

[22] "The Wars Over Evolution," Richard C. Lewontin, in *The New York Review of Books*, Vol. 52, No. 16, October 20, 2005; accessible at: http://www.nybooks.com/articles/18363.

[23] *The Politically Incorrect Guide™ to Science*, by Tom Bethell (Regnery Publishing, Inc., 2005); pages 219–21.

[24] From the website, "Evolution Happens" (Donald J. Tosaw, Jr., 1999–2006); accessible at: http://www.evolutionhappens.net. See especially the response to the query, "Isn't evolution inconsistent with the Second Law of Thermodynamics?"

[25] From the website discussion, "Darwin's Great Tautology: Discussion of Two Fatal Defects in His Theory of Evolution," May 1997; accessible at: http://www.tdtone.org/darwin/Darwin1.htm. See also Bethell; page 208.

[26] Colby; see especially the section entitled, "Mechanisms That Decrease Genetic Variation."

[27] "FAQs: What Is Intelligent Design?" (Beliefnet, Inc., 2006); accessible from: http://www.beliefnet.com/story/166/story_16641_1.html.

[28] "Is Intelligent Design Biblical?" by Denis R. Alexander; accessible at: http://www.cis.org.uk/resources/articles/article_archive/EN_IDarticle.pdf.

[29] From the essay, "In Defense of Intelligent Design," by William A. Dembski of the Center for Science and Theology, Southern Baptist Theological Seminary; pages 1–2, 8.

[30] See some of the ID arguments discussed in Bethell; pages 199–214.

[31] "Science and Design," by William A. Dembski, in *First Things*, October 1998; accessible at: http://www.firstthings.com/ftissues/ft9810/dembski.html.

[32] Alexander; "Is Intelligent Design Biblical?"

[33] Alexander; "Is Intelligent Design Biblical?"

[34] "Is Evolution Atheistic?" by Denis R. Alexander, first published in *Evangelicals Now*, January 2003; reproduced with permission on the official website of Christians in Science at: http://www.cis.org.uk/resources/articles/article_archive/evolution_atheistic.htm.

[35] *Finding Darwin's God: A Scientist's Search for Common Ground Between God and Evolution*, by Kenneth R. Miller (Harper Perennial, 2000); pages 258, 270.

[36] *Baker Theological Dictionary of the Bible*, edited by Walter A. Elwell (Baker Books, 1996); page 651.

CHAPTER 5
THE UNIVERSE

Focus: This chapter discusses the vastness of the universe and the encounters between cosmological science and religious belief.

Glory Above the Heavens

When I served my first pastorate in Pope County, Illinois, I lived about 15 miles out in the country. Each night, without the artificial light of a town, I enjoyed a very beautiful view of the starry sky. I truly gained a sense of God's glory, not to mention feelings of awe and humility.

Read Psalm 8:3-4 again. What thoughts or feelings do you have when you look up into the sky on a starry night? What questions emerge for you when you look at the heavens?

A few years later, when I served an Arizona congregation, I was privileged to tour the Lowell Observatory in Flagstaff. There, Percival Lowell had studied Mars for many years. Another astronomer at the observatory discovered evidence of the expanding nature of the universe. And in 1930, yet another astronomer discovered the planet Pluto at the observatory. During my visit, I was thrilled to see Saturn's rings.

Cosmological science does not threaten as many people as does evolutionary science. Nevertheless, this area of study has contained interesting encounters with religious beliefs.

The World of the Bible

The Bible gives us an ancient view of the cosmos. Defenders of the literal sense of the Bible usually refer to Genesis 1 rather than other Scriptures that reflect an ancient cosmology. The Bible speaks as if the sun orbits the earth: "The sun rises and the sun goes down, and hurries to the place where it rises" (Ecclesiastes 1:5). In Joshua 10:12-14, the sun and the moon both stopped in the sky as a favorite omen while Joshua and the Israelites fought the Amorites. The Bible depicts the earth as secured on pillars (1 Samuel 2:8b; Job 9:6), with a dome (firmament) above (Psalm 19:1), and the land is spread out upon the waters (Psalm 136:6). In Psalm 104:5, God has "set the earth on its foundations, so that it shall never be shaken." But in Job, the earth is not held aloft but "hangs . . . upon nothing" (26:7).

> Read Joshua 10:12-14; 1 Samuel 2:8b; Job 9:6; 26:7; Psalms 19:1; 104:5; 136:6; and Ecclesiastes 1:5. What do these Scriptures say to you about the universe? About God?

We miss the point if we focus upon the literal images and forget the main purpose: the glory of God. Psalm 19 declares, "The heavens are telling the glory of God; and the firmament proclaims his handiwork. Day to day pours forth speech, and night to night declares knowledge" (verses 1-2). The "speech" of the cosmos is not in terms of human language but is yet clear throughout the world (verses 3-4).

> In previous centuries, it was easy for people to think of our world as the focus of God's concern. Do you think that has changed, now that we know the earth is a tiny, tiny place within the vastness of the universe? Why do you think people become upset about evolution but not astronomy, since both sciences contradict a literal reading of Genesis?

The Book of Job reflects on the cosmos and the world. "Can you, like [God], spread out the skies, hard as a molten mirror?" (37:18). "Can you bind the chains of the Pleiades, or loose the cords of Orion? . . . Do you know the ordinances of the heavens? Can you establish their rule on earth?" (38:31, 33). These and other verses (28:25-28; 36:27-33; and 38:22-41) concern the inability of human beings to

> If you're studying this book as a group, divide into smaller groups and look up the verses cited in this section: Job 28:25-28; 36:27-33; 37:18; and 38:22-41. Discuss the various biblical images of the earth and the universe. Create a group sketch of the universe based upon your reading and discussion.

comprehend works and purposes of God. The author of Job finds the vastness of God's work daunting.

The author of Psalm 8 contemplated the heavens with the naked eye. How much more do we find astonishing the heavens and stars based on what we now know! How much more do we ask, "What are human beings that you are mindful of them, mortals that you care for them?" (verse 4).

This *Is* Rocket Science

Do you know the nearest and most distant stars? The Sun is the closest star, 93 million miles away. The next closest is Proxima Centuri, about 25 trillion miles (4.3 light-years) away.[1] The Andromeda Galaxy is the farthest object that we can see with the naked eye, about 2.2 million light-years away.[2] In 2004, scientists in Europe discovered a galaxy over 13 billion light-years away.[3] The speed of light is 299,792,458 meters per second

> The well-known author Ray Bradbury wrote a story called "The Man," in which a space traveler visits another world. Jesus had visited that world but had recently departed. The traveler sets out to find Jesus; perhaps he could encounter Jesus on yet another world. The story can be found in *Bradbury Stories* (Harper Perennial, 2005).
>
> In your opinion, do you think Jesus would visit life on other worlds? If so, would he say or do the same things? Is it important that Jesus' life and work was tied in with the history of the Jewish people here on earth?

(in a vacuum), or about 186,282 miles per second. A light-year is the distance that light travels in a year, approximately 5,895,696,000,000 miles, or about 9,460,800,000,000 kilometers.[4] If you wanted to travel to Proxima Centuri, the journey would require traveling at 186,282 miles per second for over four years. (The Space Shuttle, in comparison, travels five miles per second.)[5]

Do you like science fiction and speculative fiction? Many science fiction works have religious themes. For a list of novels and authors, check the site http://www.adherents.com/lit/sf_rel.html.

Also check the entries "religion" and "messiah" in *The Encyclopedia of Science Fiction*, second edition, edited by John Clute and Peter Nicholls (St. Martin's Press, 1993).

If you wanted to travel to Andromeda . . . well, pack your favorite snacks, because even if light-speed travel were possible, you would have to travel many, many years to reach the stars.

The Earth's Place in the Heavens

A few Greek thinkers had "modern" ideas about the cosmos. For instance, Aristarchus, in the 200's B.C., believed the sun to be the center of our system.[6] But most ancient thinkers derived their conclusions from observation: the stars, the sun, and the planets move around the earth.

The astronomical theories of Claudius Ptolemy (ca. 100–170) remained sound until the 1500's. Ptolemy's model of the universe placed the earth near the center of an eccentric circle, around which the sun and the planets move. The planets make "epicycles" around the earth, that is, looping orbits which brought them closer and then farther from the earth.[7]

Have you ever had to make a major decision, or perform a major duty, based on incomplete information? What happened? How did the situation turn out? What did you learn from the experience?

Ptolemy's model is a good example of how a scientific theory is suitable for a certain period of time but eventually is superseded as new data is found. Was Ptolemy wrong? Technically, yes. But in another sense he was not wrong—in that his mathematically-sophisticated theories satisfactorily interpreted the data that was available to him.

70

The first astronomical advancements in centuries came in the Renaissance era; although interestingly, an earlier writer, Martianus Capella of the fourth and fifth centuries, believed that some of the planets orbited the sun.[8] Nicolaus Copernicus (1473–1543) was a Polish thinker who developed afresh the theory of a heliocentric (sun-centered) planetary system. He resurrected the idea of the earth's motion on an axis, with the earth moving around the sun between Venus and Mars, and with the moon moving around the earth. Interestingly, Copernicus was also a Roman

> We're accustomed to thinking that heaven is "in the sky" and hell is "down below." Modern astronomy and geology give us a very different picture of the earth and sky. Where do you think heaven and hell exist? Do you believe they're literal places? How do you understand heaven and hell? An interesting book is Randy Alcorn's *Heaven* (Tyndale House Publishers, 2004).

Catholic official whose experiments partly had to do with predicting the date of Easter with greater accuracy.[9]

The Poster Child for Religion-Science Conflict

Another scientist, Johannes Kepler (1571–1630), postulated that the planets orbited elliptically around the sun.[10] But Galileo Galilei (1564–1642) made significant strides—and trouble. Galileo heard of a child's toy, made of lenses in a tube, which brought objects closer when one looked in an end. Galileo made a telescope of his own and eventually discovered moons around the planet Jupiter.[11]

Galileo's discovery showed a problem in the science of the time. Many scientific conclusions were derived deductively from Aristotle's philosophy and also from theological assertions. People believed there were seven heavenly bodies—the sun, the moon, Mercury, Venus, Mars, Jupiter, and Saturn. Furthermore, seven was a symbolic number used frequently in the Bible; therefore God had created the universe to reflect the number seven.[12] But in the new empirical method, typified by Kepler, one began not with theological or philosophical truths, but from observed facts.[13]

Galileo was examined by the Inquisition in 1615–16 and was actually tried in 1633. He was forbidden to teach his scientific ideas; but contrary to popular myth, he was never tortured or threatened with death. An earlier thinker, Giordano Bruno (1548–1600), was a controversial astronomer, excommunicated by Catholics and Protestants alike prior to his execution for heretical teachings about the nature of Christ.[14]

Galileo's case is complicated. Copernicus' ideas had not been condemned by the Church; but by the time of Galileo, the Catholic Church was in a defensive situation in the aftermath of the Protestant Reformation. Perhaps even more importantly, Galileo, who could be arrogant, had put forth his theories in a way that caused the Pope, a friend of Galileo's, to feel betrayed and mocked. Galileo's case, and to a lesser extent Bruno's, have been used by writers as evidence that religion necessarily takes a defensive stance against scientific advancement. The Church gave itself a metaphorical black eye that remains today.

> Read more about the cases of Galileo and Bruno in an encyclopedia or one of the history books that are cited at the end of Chapter 3.
>
> Have you ever been in trouble by authorities when you knew you were right? Did you ever feel vindicated, or did you have to just "move on"?

Galileo also developed profoundly new descriptions of motion. Aristotle, and scientists after him, believed that objects fall at a speed proportional to their weight. This makes sense, after all: drop an anvil and a feather and see what happens. Galileo showed that air resistance causes the apparent discrepancy; but in a vacuum, all objects fall at the same rate, regardless of their weight.[15]

A Religious Man Revolutionizes Science

Who are the greatest scientific geniuses? Among the many contenders are Galileo and, in our own time, Stephen Hawking. But as independent filmmaker and science author Thomas Levenson puts it, there are really only two at the finish line: Newton and Einstein.[16]

Why is Sir Isaac Newton (1642–1727) important for us to know? Newton was able to explain natural laws and physics, without using philosophical and religious explanations, thus revolutionizing science and opening up new areas of discovery and research.

Based upon previous mathematical work, Newton perfected the field of mathematics called calculus. He also discovered principles of color and light; by using a prism, he showed that light is a combination of colors, and the colors we see in nature originate in the light spectrum. He perfected the telescope, using mirrors instead of several lenses.[17]

In addition to his discoveries in mathematics and optics, Newton developed the principles of gravity. (He actually made these discoveries within 18 months in 1665–67, when he was in his twenties.[18] He did not publish them for several years, however.) Newton showed that the weight of any object is the gravitational pull upon that object. Objects attract other objects, and the force occurs on a line between the centers of the object.

For sphere-like objects such as planets, this force can be calculated with a formula: $F=Gm_1m_2/r^2$ (or the mass of the first object, multiplied by the mass of the second object, multiplied by the constant number "G" (6.67×10^{-11}), all divided by the distance between the objects squared).[19] Newton's theory explained the orbits of planets and their moons. Our own moon, for instance, continually falls toward the earth because of gravitational force.[20]

> Gerald L. Schroeder is an Israeli physicist whose book, *The Hidden Face of God: How Science Reveals the Ultimate Truth* (Touchstone, 2001), traces several aspects of complexity and harmony within the natural world. Without arguing for a particular religious dogma, Schroeder writes with a contagious sense of wonder at the wisdom that pervades the universe.

As we saw earlier, Galileo theorized that objects in a vacuum fall at the same rate. Newton was able to formulate that acceleration with the formula $F=ma$ (the force of gravity equals the mass of the object multiplied by its acceleration).[21]

Newton was a very religious person; although he was anti-Catholic and, like Galileo, could be very arrogant. (Coincidentally, Newton was born the same year Galileo died.) Newton believed in the inerrancy of the Bible and in the biblical prophecies, yet he did not believe in the Trinity.[22] When you survey Newton's achievements, you appreciate his importance for science and for popular imagination, too. Here was a scientist who used his knowledge, imagination,

> Do additional research on Isaac Newton in books, encyclopedias, or online. Share the results of your research with the group. What in your research stood out for you? What connections can you make between the Christian faith and discoveries of Newton?

observations, and skill to discover important truths about nature. To many,

Newton had discovered principles of the universe that only God had known—and he did so without recourse to the Scriptures or traditional natural philosophy. Little wonder that the poet Alexander Pope (1688–1744) wrote of Newton in his famous couplet:

Nature, and Nature's Laws lay hid in Night.
God said, *Let Newton be!* and All was *Light*.[23]

Einstein

Closer to our own time, Albert Einstein (1879–1955) is a paragon of scientific genius. His appearance, with his gentle expression and wild hair, has become a popular icon. Even Einstein's name stands metaphorically for anyone with exceptional ability; he himself told someone, humorously, "I'm no Einstein."[24] Religious in a way, but not in the sense of believing in a personal God, Einstein became a notable moral voice in the twentieth century for both Zionism and international peace.[25] His famous statement, "God does not play dice," has less to do with spirituality than the certainty of natural laws.[26]

Like Newton, Einstein was in his twenties when he developed his key theories. In fact, he developed some of his theories in his spare time while working as a patent examiner. Beginning in 1905 when he was 26, he made significant contributions to quantum theory, described light as both particles and waves, and proved the connection of matter and energy by the now-famous formula $E=mc^2$ (energy equals mass multiplied by the speed of light squared).

> Have you ever known a "genius"? What does that person do for a living? How does that person use his or her exceptional abilities?

During the ensuing years, Einstein also made other notable advancements in quantum theory, developed the special theory of relativity needed to describe the motion of fast-moving objects, and showed how gravity shapes both time and space.[27] One of his many key formulas that is quite sophisticated is $G_{\mu\nu}=8\pi T_{\mu\nu}$ (the curvature of space-time in any part of the universe equals the distribution of energy and matter in that part).[28]

In Newton's theories, space and time are absolute. According to Einstein's "special theory of relativity," distance and time vary depending upon the movement of one object relative to something else. If an object passes you lengthwise, for instance, it will be shorter in length than if it were at rest. Similarly a clock will run more slowly if it passes you rapidly. Newton's theories remain sound when applied to everyday objects, but as objects move at speeds that approach the speed of light, Einstein's theories must be used. If we were traveling at the speed of light, time would stop for us.[29]

In Einstein's general theory of relativity, gravity and acceleration affect space and time. For instance, you feel pulled back (and thus feel temporarily heavier) when you're accelerating in a forward direction. Similarly the sun's gravity affects space and time; close to the sun, space curves and time slows. Einstein's theories explain discrepancies in the orbit of Mercury (the planet closest to the sun) that Newton was unable to explain with his gravitational laws.[30] General relativity was also confirmed in 1919 when, during a solar eclipse, an experiment showed that light from stars bend due to the sun's gravity.[31]

> How do space ships in science fiction stories travel enormous distances within a few hours or days? In *Star Trek*, ships travel by the "warp drive." Warp drive is not actually propulsion but is a warping of the space-time continuum. Because of the annihilation-reaction of matter and antimatter in the ship's "warp core" engine (a reaction that is regulated by dilithium crystals), a ship like the *Enterprise* can expand space-time behind the ship and contract it in front, thus allowing for faster-than-light-speed travel, as explained by Lawrence M. Krauss in his book, *The Physics of Star Trek* (Basic Books, 1995); pages 54–56.

As with other theories, Einstein's were excellent because they could be used to predict and verify experimental results. Einstein's ideas helped later scientists show that the universe is expanding. His ideas were also important in the 1930's as scientists demonstrated the theoretical existence of black holes.[32]

> Do additional research on Einstein in books, encyclopedias, or online. Share the results of your research with the group. What in your research stood out for you? What connections can you make between the Christian faith and discoveries of Einstein?

Einstein hoped to find a "theory of everything"("T.O.E.") that united theories of subatomic particles, energy, force, and so on. He never found that theory.[33] The author Stephen Hawking, well known for his popular books and his courageous struggle with ALS, is but one scientist interested in finding a unifying theory.[34] (Here's another trivia fact for you: Hawking was born January 8, 1942, which was the 300th anniversary of Galileo's death!)[35] David Wilkinson of St. Johns College, University of Durham, a Methodist minister and astrophysicist, has explored many of these issues in his book, *God, Time and Stephen Hawking.*

> According to Heisenberg's uncertainty principle (which Einstein didn't like), you cannot simultaneously measure the position and momentum of a subatomic particle. This principle is a cornerstone of quantum physics, the science of measuring the properties of subatomic objects.[35]

Religion and Science

What effects did the theories of Newton and Einstein have upon religion?

Newton believed that God remained actively involved in the universe, for instance, in the movement of the planets. But his ideas caused some philosophers and scientists to downplay God's ongoing providence. If the universe was so perfectly formed according to mathematical laws and predictable principles, does God need to intervene in the natural world? A clockmaker has little or no involvement, for instance, once the clock is constructed. So it is with God and God's marvelous creation. Scientists and philosophers in the late 1600's and through the 1700's became interested in "rational religion," a belief in God that drastically downplayed miracles, elevated reason, and natural laws.[37]

Newton himself tried to retain God's providential involvement in the universe. Even though God's care could not be expressed mathematically, the universe nevertheless relied upon God's direction.[38]

Some have worried that the relativity theory, along with the uncertainty principle, promotes relativism—the philosophy that truth is subjective. In fact, early in the twentieth century some church officials criticized Einstein for propagating atheism and relativism.[39] True, Einstein's theories state that a phenomenon depends upon the position of the observer. But he maintained that the physical laws remain constant and the speed of light remains an absolute standard; his theories, he said, were really about absolutes. As Ian Barbour points out, Einstein's theories also encourage interrelationships within the universe, since space and time, and mass and energy, are now connected.[40]

Einstein's status as a moral spokesman and pop culture icon makes him appealing in popular imagination. Also, his theory of an expanding universe provides, for some people, a scientific basis for creation.

> What feelings or thoughts occur to you as you consider the theory of an expanding universe?

The Big Bang

According to the "Big Bang" theory, the universe was originally a "singularity," or a single point. It was not a singularity *in* space; rather space existed in the singularity. Scientists have no explanation for the origin of that singularity. But about 13.7 billion years ago, the singularity expanded very rapidly. (One common misconception of this theory is that the "bang" was an explosion rather than a sudden expansion.)[41] The expansion sent out neutrons, which, as they decayed, released free protons and electrons which then bonded, providing deuterium ("heavy hydrogen") and helium, and soon regular hydrogen.[42]

Several thinkers helped develop the theory. In 1927, Georges Lemaître, a Belgian priest, postulated an ancient explosion.[43] Edwin Hubble, for whom the famous telescope is named, discovered that galaxies are moving away from us in proportion to their distances. (The distance of a galaxy, times its velocity, equals the age of the universe. Thus, we get the figure of 13.7 billion years.) A galaxy three times as far from us moves three times faster. Hubble also noted that the universe expands in all directions. In 1964, the astronomers Arno Penzias and Robert Wilson discovered "noise" in space that came from all directions; this noise is radiation remaining from the "bang."[44] Astronomer Fred Hoyle coined the term "Big Bang" in 1950, albeit sarcastically, since he disagreed with the theory.[45]

Does the Big Bang conform to Genesis? The theory postulates a definite beginning to the universe, and therefore is more congenial to the Genesis account than, say, a theory that the universe is eternal, without beginning or end. Like Thomas Aquinas' famous five ways (as discussed in Chapter 3), the "bang" seems to be a way to demonstrate a god at the beginning of time.

What caused the Big Bang? This question, too, invites theological speculation. As we saw in Chapter 4, it's possible to embrace evolutionary theory as a suitable explanation for how God creates and preserves life. Similarly, the Big Bang seems to provide an explanation for how God caused the cosmos to be.

Others think this assertion is premature. The Big Bang is a theory, a model for explaining natural phenomena. If we, too, say that God used the Big Bang to create the universe, where will we be if the theory is drastically altered or replaced someday by the scientific community?

> Is the Big Bang proof of God? Do you find it theologically congenial or not? Find more information about this theory as well as alternative theories.

Genesis portrays a more deliberate, straightforward plan of God, focusing upon life and matter on earth. David Wilkinson notes that "such an attempt to prove the existence of God often leads to a picture of God closer to deism rather than the Bible. . . . Creation is not a single initial act, but the bringing into being and moment by moment keeping in being of the whole Universe (Colossians 1:15-17; Hebrews 1:3)."[46]

A Sense of Wonder

Peter J. Gomes tells the story of a turn-of-the-nineteenth-century preacher in New England who preached a yearly sermon on recent astronomical discoveries. When asked why he preached such a sermon, he is reported to have said that astronomical discoveries broadened his view of God.[47]

Do you feel the same way about science? Evolutionary theory and biology invoke awe in many people who appreciate the amazing intricacies and beauty of the natural world; cosmological science similarly inspires awe and reverence. Go outside tonight and look at the heavens. If you live in a city, go out to the country sometime and look at the stars again. Gain a deeper sense of the wonders of God's universe!

Closing
Read Psalm 8 aloud as you did in the opening. Thank God for caring about you intimately, though you're a tiny part of the universe. Ask the Lord to help you stay strong as you deal with the various challenges and situations of your life at the moment.

For Further Reading

A Brief History of Time, by Stephen W. Hawking (Bantam Books, 1996).

The Comforting Whirlwind: God, Job, and the Scale of Creation, by Bill McKibben (Cowley Publications, 2005).

God, Time and Stephen Hawking, by David Wilkinson (Monarch Books, 2001).

The Physics of Star Trek, by Lawrence M. Krauss (Basic Books, 1995).

Notes

[1] From the online edition of *The American Heritage® Dictionary of the English Language*, fourth edition (Houghton Mifflin Company, 2000); accessible at: http://www.bartleby.com/61/39/S0883900.html. See also the report, "The Nearest Stars to Earth," presented by Bill Baity of the Center for Astrophysics and Space Sciences; available at: http://casswww.ucsd.edu/public/nearest.html.

[2] *The American Heritage® Dictionary of the English Language*; accessible at: http://www.bartleby.com/61/31/A0293100.html.

[3] From the article "Universe's Farthest Galaxy Found," *Associated Press*, March 1, 2004; accessible from the CBS News website: http://www.cbsnews.com/stories/2004-/03/01/tech/main603096.shtml.

[4] See "light-year," from the online HighBeam™ Encyclopedia (HighBeam™ Research, Inc., 2006); accessible from: http://www.encyclopedia.com/doc/1E1-lightyea.html.

[5] See "Speed of a Space Shuttle," from the online resource Hypertextbook.com (Glenn Elert, 1987–2006); available from: http://hypertextbook.com/facts/2001/InnaSokolyanskaya1.shtml.

[6] *Science and Religion, 400 B.C. to A.D. 1550: From Aristotle to Copernicus*, by Edward Grant (Greenwood Press, 2004); page 82.

[7] Grant; pages 78–82. *A History of Western Philosophy: Hobbes to Hume*, by W. T. Jones, second edition (Harcourt, Brace & World, Inc., 1969); page 92.

[8] Grant; page 139.

[9] *Science and Religion, 1450–1900: From Copernicus to Darwin*, by Richard G. Olson (Greenwood Press, 2004); page 7.

[10] From the official NASA *Kepler Mission* webpage; available at: http://kepler.nasa.gov-/johannes/index.html.

[11] Jones; page 99.

[12] Jones; page 101.

[13] Jones; pages 101–02.

[14] "Giordano Bruno: The Forgotten Philosopher," by Dr. John J. Kessler (Internet Infidels, Inc., 1995–2006); available at: http://www.infidels.org/library/historical/john_kessler/-giordano_bruno.html.

[15] See the lecture, "Galileo's Laws of Motion," from the website of the University of Oregon Department of Physics; available at: http://jersey.uoregon.edu/~js/ast221/lectures/lec07.html.

[16] From the article "Genius Among Geniuses," by Thomas Levenson; accessible from NOVA on the PBS website, "Einstein's Big Idea," at: http://www.pbs.org/wgbh/nova/einstein/genius/.

[17] *World Book Encyclopedia*, Vol. 14, (World Book, Inc., 2004); pages 388–90.

[18] *World Book Encyclopedia*, Vol. 14; page 388.

[19] See formula on "Tutor4physics.com"; available at: http://tutor4physics.com/formulas.htm.

[20] *World Book Encyclopedia*, Vol. 14; pages 388–89.

[21] See note 19 above.

[22] See the essay, "Sir Isaac Newton," from the website of the Lucasian Chair of Mathematics at Cambridge University; accessible at: http://www.lucasianchair.org/newton.html. See also *A Brief History of Time*, by Stephen W. Hawking (Bantam, 1996); pages 196–97.

[23] *The Poems of Alexander Pope*, edited by John Butt (Yale University Press, 1963); page 808.

[24] "Why We Love Einstein," in *Seed*, October/November 2005; page 71.

[25] From an interview with Harvard University professor Gerald Holton, "Albert Einstein: Religiously Scientific," by Anne Reilly, from the online edition of *Science & Theology News*, May 16, 2005.

[26] Quotation available from: http://www.brainyquote.com/quotes/quotes/a/alberteins136-883.html (BrainyMedia.com, 2006).

[27] See note 16 above.

[28] See "Einstein Field Equations," from the Wolfram Research website (Wolfram Research, Inc., 2006); accessible at: http://scienceworld.wolfram.com/physics/EinsteinFieldEquations.html.

[29] See "The Special Theory of Relativity," by John L. Safko (J. L. Safko, 2004); accessible from: http://astro.physics.sc.edu/selfpacedunits/unit56.html.

[30] "Precession of the Perihelion of Mercury," by Dr. Jose Wudka of University of California Riverside; available at: http://physics.ucr.edu/~wudka/Physics7/Notes_www/node98.html.

[31] From the article, "Relativity and the Cosmos," by Alan Lightman; accessible from NOVA on the PBS website at: http://www.pbs.org/wgbh/nova/einstein/relativity/.

[32] See note 31 above.

[33] From the article, "A Theory of Everything?" by Brian Greene; accessible from NOVA on the PBS website at: http://www.pbs.org/wgbh/nova/elegant/everything.html.

[34] *God, Time and Stephen Hawking*, by David Wilkinson (Monarch Books, 2001); pages 99–101.

[35] From the website of Stephen Hawking; accessible from: http://www.hawking.org.uk/-home/hindex.html.

[36] From "Werner Heisenberg and Albert Einstein," by Gerald Holton, from the website of the American Institute of Physics (AIP, 2006); available at: http://www.aip.org/pt/vol-53/iss-7/p38.html.

[37] *Science and Religion: A Historical Introduction*, edited by Gary B. Ferngren (Johns Hopkins University Press, 2002); page 326. *Religion and Science: Historical and Contemporary Issues*, by Ian G. Barbour (HarperCollins, 1997); pages 19–24.

[38] Olson; pages 123–24.

[39] See note 25 above.

[40] Barbour; page 180.

[41] From the article, "Big Bang Theory—The Premise" (AllAboutScience.org, 2002–06); accessible from the AllAboutScience.org website at: http://www.big-bang-theory.com/.

[42] From "The Big Bang: It Sure Was BIG!" by Chris LaRocco and Blair Rothstein of the University of Michigan (The Regents of the University of Michigan, 2006); accessible at: http://www.umich.edu/~gs265/bigbang.htm.

[43] "'A Day Without Yesterday': Georges Lemaître & the Big Bang," by Mark Midbon (Commonweal, 2000); available from the website of the Catholic Educator's Resource Center at: http://catholiceducation.org/articles/science/sc0022.html.

[44] See note 42 above.

[45] See note 41 above.

[46] From "The Absence of God or a Surer Path to God?" by David Wilkinson, in *Borderlands* (St. Johns College, 2002).

[47] *The Good Book: Reading the Bible With Mind and Heart*, by Peter J. Gomes (HarperSanFrancisco, 1996); page 312.

CHAPTER 6
MODERN MEDICINE

Focus: This session looks at scientific advances in medicine and the theological meanings of being human.

Gathering
Greet one another. Catch up on events since you last met. Read together Psalm 30, a psalm of thanksgiving for healing.

On the Examining Table

You think the universe is impressive? Listen to this. According to author Owen Flanagan, there are approximately 10^{87} elementary particles in the universe. (By comparison, one trillion is 10^{12}.) Compare that with the $10^{100,000,000,000,000}$ possible distinct brain states produced by the 100 billion (10^{11}) neurons in *your* own personal nervous system.[1] You yourself are an amazing universe of neurological activity, intricate functioning, and genetic complexity.

Unfortunately, sometimes that "universe" breaks down; we face illness. During those times, we seek modern medical care, but we also beseech God for help and healing. Psalm 30 is a classic song of thanksgiving for healing. When sick, the psalmist even "reasoned" with God; what benefit would be the psalmist's death (verses 8-9)? Once healed, the psalmist rejoices.

We know the feeling! I remember a time of hospitalization when I felt upset at the uncertainty of my prognosis and the various indignities, from the endless battery of tests, to the doctor who chewed me out for misunderstanding a procedure. When I finally was pronounced fine, I rejoiced like that psalmist!

To some religious people, evolutionary theory reduces life to a blind process; life has no meaning other than the survival of genes. As we have seen, science is an investigative and descriptive practice and does not address questions of meaning; and evolutionary theory does not necessarily have to lead to materialism and atheism. But one risk of science is that *everything* becomes potentially an object for investigation and description.

This reductive tendency of science becomes more personal in the field of medicine. You can question or embrace evolutionary theory, but eventually you or someone close to you will be seriously ill someday and need a doctor. Will you or your loved one feel treated like a person? Medical procedures can turn us into "objects" for examination and treatment, but we are more than just our physical bodies.

> If the subject isn't too personal, discuss experiences you've had with illness and hospitalization. How did God work in your life during that situation? Did you feel like God was very close or absent?

Body, Soul, and Spirit Together

Perhaps you grew up, as I did, in a tradition that emphasized "salvation of the soul." We tend to think of the soul as an eternal nature that is separate from the body; human nature is beset with sin and destined for death, but our spiritual nature, our souls, live eternally through God's grace. Passages such as 2 Corinthians 5:1-10 seem to provide scriptural warrant to this "dualism," that is, a twofold model of human nature as body and soul. We are also indebted to Descartes and Kant (discussed in Chapter 3) for their very influential, philosophical divisions of mind and body and of reason and reality.

> Read 2 Corinthians 5:1-10. How do you respond to Paul's ideas about human existence? Identify the images in this Scripture. What images would you use to describe human existence?

But the Bible gives us a more unified picture of human nature. In Chapter 3, we saw that the word "heart" in the Bible is a metaphor for several qualities of human being: reason, will, desires, and so on. Similarly, we do not see sharp distinctions within the biblical depictions of body, soul, and spirit.

The word that is translated "spirit" (in Greek *pneuma*, in Hebrew *ruah*) can also be translated as "breath." Likewise, the Hebrew word sometimes translated as "soul," *nepheš*, originally meant "throat" and came to mean "life" or "vitality." The Greek word for soul is *psychē*. We still use versions of some of these words in English, as in "pneumonia" and "psychology." The word "psychosomatic" combines the Greek word *psychē* with the Greek word *sōma*, which means "body." Dr. Joel B. Green, professor of New Testament Interpretation at Asbury Theological Seminary, notes that *nepheš* points to the biblical model of human beings as whole, and claims that in the Bible, "body" refers to the human person as a whole, as do the words "soul" and "spirit."[3]

> "Beam me up!" Lawrence M. Krauss, in his book *The Physics of Star Trek*, notes that the *Star Trek* transporter machine raises an interesting theological question. The transporter disassembles, transmits, and then reassembles the person; but what happens to the person's soul during this process? For that matter, are a person's dreams, memories, and hopes all transported, too? If so, that suggests that a person is nothing more than a collection of atoms, and our spiritual nature is simply a function of our physical nature. Krauss notes that the *Star Trek* episodes wisely avoid these questions directly.[2] How do you respond to these questions?

We also tend to think of the soul as something unique to humans. But interestingly, the word *nepheš* is used in Genesis 1:30 to refer to the life of animals as well. The concept of the image of God (*imago Dei*) is, biblically, the really distinctive aspect of human beings. Genesis 1:26 states that we are created in God's image. According to Dr. Green, Paul takes up this concept (found relatively seldom in the Old Testament) and applies it to Christ (2 Corinthians 4:4; Colossians1:15) and to "the conformation of human beings into the 'image of Christ' (Romans 8:29; 1 Corinthians 15:49; 2 Corinthians 3:18)."[4] Dr. Green writes that the idea of the image of God "emphasizes the human's covenantal relationships with other

> Form teams of two or three. Read 2 Corinthians 4:4; Colossians 1:15; Romans 8:29; 2 Corinthians 3:18; and 1 Corinthians 15:35-58. What do these Scriptures say to you about human existence? Do you think of yourself as a soul, a body, or a combination of both? What do you think is the soul?
>
> Read together Jeremiah 1:5. This verse refers to Jeremiah, but does it apply to other people? How so? How does God's intimate knowledge of us define us as human beings?

humans, and situates the human family in meaningful relationship with the whole cosmos."[5]

Our salvation, then, is a salvation of our whole person. Paul calls this a mystery (1 Corinthians 15:51), but we will also be embodied in the world to come (15:35-58).

The theologian Paul Tillich notes that when faith talks about the soul, it "is not interfering at all with the scientific rejection of the concept of the soul. . . . The truth of man's eternal meaning lies in a dimension other than the truth of adequate psychological concepts."[6]

> What does it mean to you to consider human existence as a unity of physical, psychological, and spiritual aspects? How would you illustrate each of these aspects of human existence?

This has importance for religion and science. To think of humans as a unity of physical, psychological, and spiritual aspects—and to think of humans as existing in unity and relationship with each other and with other life in the world—comes closer to the biblical model and provides some fruitful avenues in the dialogue with science, which tends to locate our identity in genetics and neurology.[7]

Miracles

A point of conflict between science and religion is the miracle. We call something a "miracle" when something, indeed, causes us to wonder and to be awe-inspired, but which is actually in the natural course of things. The birth of our daughter was a miracle in this sense; she was born through the natural reproductive process. But to behold a new life in such a way brings a sense of wonder—and wonderful happiness and gratitude to God.

We also use the term miracle to describe something wonderful that happens but which cannot exactly be explained. During my wife's pregnancy, for instance, her blood test indicated possible abnormali-

> Have you ever seen or experienced a healing miracle? What happened? Do you think the miracle was potentially explainable, or completely inexplicable, by science?

ties in our daughter. We all prayed, and the next blood test indicated no abnormalities. There was possibly an adequate scientific explanation for what happened, but that was less relevant compared to the prayerful relationship we had with God in that situation.

Similarly, we claim as miracles things that may *someday* be explained scientifically but cannot be yet. This is an area where we need to be careful as religious people, because we open our religious truth-claims to possible repudiation. I may say that it is a "miracle" that people act selflessly, for instance. But biologists are already researching the genetic roots of selfless behavior.[8]

There are also miracles that *are* actual miracles but are part of the "everyday" reality of religious life. The power of the Holy Spirit in my life, my eternal salvation, the reconciliation that Christ has accomplished between us and God and among human beings (Ephesians 2:15-20), the spiritual power granted to us in the sacraments, the serendipitous occurrences that happen in our daily lives when we seek God's help and guidance— these are really the most important miracles of all. None of us can have all our prayers for healing answered, but these miracles already have been given to us.

> Jesus came to bear our diseases, in fulfillment of the prophecies (Matthew 8:17). Read the Gospels and list the miracles that Jesus performed. Do you find any miracles that might be explainable from a scientific viewpoint? Which ones? Which of Jesus' miracles defy scientific explanation? Would your faith be lessened if any of Jesus' miracles could be explained scientifically? How do you respond to scientific explanations of Jesus' miracles?
>
> Extend your study to other books of the Bible, for instance Acts or Exodus, where you find miraculous events.

Finally, miracles are amazing occurrences that cannot be explained through normal scientific laws or theories. John calls Jesus' miracles "signs" that help us believe (John 20:30-31), proofs and proclamations of God's truth. Certainly those miracles, like the transformation of water to wine and the raising of Lazarus, resist scientific explanation (John 4:46; 11–12). When people asked Jesus for "showy" miracles, he told them that the greatest miracle of all—his resurrection—would have to suffice (Matthew 12:39). Even miracles cannot guarantee belief (12:43-45).

> Study Psalms 6; 30; 31; 38; 41; 71; and 88, which all have to do with healing. How do the psalmists pray when they are sick? What do they ask for? Are they bold or reticent when they pray? What do they do if or when healing comes?

This can be a painful subject, because deserving people do not experience healing miracles. Obviously miracles don't happen on demand, the way I get hot water from my faucet. But miracles also do not happen because of the strength of a person's faith. Peter's friends prayed for him when he was imprisoned, yet they did not believe when Peter was miraculously released (Acts 12:1-17). Famously, Paul prayed for deliverance from his "thorn," but the miracle that he received (no less a miracle than healing) was strength and grace (2 Corinthians 12:7b-10).

Like "everyday" miracles, "amazing" miracles require faith and discernment. Do genuine miracles happen in a world governed by natural laws? Of course! Religious people in the era of Newton believed that the universe must be governed by discoverable, unalterable laws. But one can maintain that the natural world is a place created and governed by God, set up by God in such a way that God's power can be known and displayed. Both the natural laws of the universe and the miraculous events that we can't explain are signs of God's glory.

Looking at the natural world this way, I believe we can allow for the possibility of wonderful signs of God, while also affirming the truth and cogency of scientific explanations for most natural phenomena.

Medicine and Prayer

Since God responds to us through miracles, those both "commonplace" and unusual, can these miracles be verified by science? To put it in another way, is prayer a suitable and verifiable medical tool? While science addresses the needs and nature of the physical body, discussions have arisen in recent years whether medical science may unite the physical and spiritual aspects of human beings.

Even those who take the Bible very literally avail themselves of medical practice and do not rely upon faith and prayer alone to heal their illness. We believe that Jesus, in his time on earth, healed the sick; and he still does. But our twenty-first-century medicine is very different from that of the first century in the diagnosis and treatment of disease.

Many people argue that religious belief is an essential aspect of medicine and health. In his book, *The Faith Factor* (Penguin, 1999), Dr. Dale A. Matthews, who teaches at Georgetown University School of Medicine, argues that religious faith helps people deal with pain and anxiety, post-operative healing, and so on.

People like Dr. Matthews argue that spirituality and science belong together, that religious faith just makes good science. Practitioners don't even have to be religious experts themselves; they can ask about people's spirituality and even refer them.[9]

Others disagree. Richard P. Sloan and Larry VandeCreek, writing in *Medscape General Medicine*™, worry about spiritual coercion on the part of doctors, as well as an overstepping of boundaries. Do you really want your doctor advising you on how to pray? What if your doctor had different religious beliefs than you? Authors like Sloan and VandeCreek fear that if healthcare professionals step into the role of religious counselor, the integrity of both medicine and religion are weakened. Thus, they write, "religion doesn't need medicine to validate itself."[11]

Raymond J. Lawrence, an Episcopal priest and director of pastoral care at New York-Presbyterian Hospital/Columbia University Medical Center, wrote in an op-ed piece for the *New York Times*, "if it could ever be persuasively demonstrated that [intercessory] prayer 'works,' our religious institutions and meeting places would be degraded to a kind of commercial enterprise, like Burger King, where one expects to get what one pays for." He notes that people do derive health benefits from prayer, but "scientists should not leap to the assumption that the ruler of the universe can be mechanically requisitioned to intervene in people's suffering or health." Do you agree? If not, what are your ideas? Why do you think we offer intercessory prayer for people?[10]

Does research confirm that prayer contributes to health? Statistics differ. One study on the Internet (http://www.godandscience.org/apologetics/-prayer.html) found a statistical correlation between prayer and health. On the other hand, a recent $2.4 million study found that coronary bypass patients had more health problems when they knew people were praying for them, compared to patients who were not prayed for.[12]

Many churches are incorporating "healthcare ministries" in their programs. At the church I attend, a nurse sets up a table every few weeks and takes people's blood pressure at no cost. This past winter, our church provided flu shots for anyone who wanted one.

> Does your church have prayer ministries or other healthcare ministries for the sick? If so, what are they? If not, what might your church do to begin such ministries?

In Memphis, Tennessee, the Church Health Center provides lifestyle advice for people, as well as medical care for those with low incomes. Many churches also incorporate healing services into their worship ministries.[13]

Genetic Research

In the introduction, I discussed common anxieties about science. Should science be regulated? What if scientists conduct experiments that seem morally ambiguous? What "Pandora's box" issues should science avoid?

Genetic research is particularly fascinating. Scientists have recently mapped the human genome. The genome is comprised of a series of 3.2 billion "letters" (the letters are abbreviations for four molecules discussed below). As this series is mapped, scientists better understand the genetic process, including the development of diseases and bodily functions.

In his book, *The Hidden Face of God*, Gerald L. Schroeder notes that every microscopic cell of our bodies contain two *meters* of DNA (deoxyribonucleic acid). Chromosomes are sections of DNA that contain genetic information from both parents. Nearly all of our cells each contain four sets of 30,000 genes, which in turn are comprised of basic "nucleotide" molecules formed from the compounds adenine (A), guanine (G), cytosine (C), and thymine (T). These compounds bond together, creating the well-known double helix pattern.[14]

Each set of letters (for instance, ACG) determines the production of a certain protein called an amino acid; and each amino acid combines with other amino acids to product effects in our bodies: hormones that begin puberty, stomach digestion, insulin production, and so on. We have 20 amino acids that combine in many ways. The proteins can also combine incorrectly and thus we get cancer, mental illness, etc. Some scientists believe that the clues to intelligence and behavior lay in our proteins.

Thus genetic research appears to have many benefits. Scientists are studying the genetic roots of diseases like leukemia, breast cancer, Alzheimer's, muscular dystrophy, and others. As the understanding of genetics increases, cures for many diseases may very well result.[15]

But genetic research worries many people. While many observers support "somatic gene therapies," which change genes for the sake of addressing disease, they do not support "germ-line therapies," which create genetic changes that are passed on to future generations, or gene therapies that involve cosmetic or personal enhancement. But already parents can choose a procedure called preimplantation genetic diagnosis (PGD) for gender selection of their babies. The possibility of "designer babies" and "designer people" is very real, opening the further possibility that babies with genetic defects could be discarded. Other moral and ethical dilemmas loom ahead; for instance, will insurance companies deny coverage to people diagnosed with genetic predispositions to certain diseases?[16]

Genetic research also extends to our food production. Most of us don't realize that much of our food is genetically modified in some way.

| What fears or hopes do you have about genetic research? |

Journalist Kathleen Hart, in her book, *Eating in the Dark: America's Experiment With Genetically Engineered Food* (Pantheon Books, 2002), looks at this phenomenon with a critical eye.

Stem-Cell Research

Among the cells of our body are stem cells. Our regular cells come from stem cells—brain cells from brain stem cells, and so on. When we're adults, our stem cells are specialized to produce certain kinds of cells, but the stem cells of embryos are not yet so specialized. In fact, embryonic stem cells can produce many of the cell types that we have in our bodies. The process, presently being researched, of using stem cells to grow new cells is called therapeutic cloning, or somatic cell nuclear transfer.[17]

You hear about clones in movie and television stories; but at this writing, therapeutic cloning has been the most successful procedure. The first cloned animal, a lamb named Dolly, was born in 1996 and died in 2003. In recent years, dogs, cats, mice, and other animals have been cloned; but the process has been difficult and expensive, with unreliable success. One scientist tried to clone monkeys, but 300 attempts were all unsuccessful. Interestingly, the successfully-cloned animals have not always been "replicas" of the original animal.[18]

As recently as 1998, scientists first grew embryonic stem cells in the lab, leading to hopeful predictions that such cells could provide an ongoing source of new cells that could be used as replacement cells for persons with heart diseases, spinal-cord injuries, and more.[19]

But the ethical question points to the use of embryonic cells in this way. The embryo is destroyed so that the cells can be extracted. But is the embryo a "person"—even when it is only a collection of cells a few days old? Is it "in the image of God"? Are we "killing" a person for research when we extract the stem cells? Or are we simply using cells from a group of fertilized, dividing cells that is not at all a thinking, breathing, functioning human being?

> What thoughts or feelings do you have about stem-cell research?

Some people argue that stem-cell research would benefit many people. They argue that the blastocyst—a sphere of cells a few days old, from which stem cells can be extracted—is not a person on par with an adult suffering from cancer, spinal cord injury, Alzheimer's, or other diseases that could be addressed through stem-cell research.[20] Advancements in this medical field seem to promise to tangibly help the lives of many people. Sincere religious people cite God's concern for life and human well-being, to argue for or against the use of stem cells.

Another consideration is the development of scientific research around the world. Even though stem-cell research is strictly limited in the U.S., scientists in other parts of the world will certainly continue to seek advancements in this area. Observers worry that the U.S. will fall behind on this research and that, consequently, Americans will be denied help that could be available domestically.[21]

Still others urge caution: just because science is proceeding quickly doesn't mean that moral reflection shouldn't take place. Whether or not the embryo is a "person in the image of God," it *is* a living group of human cells that is created in order to be used for a particular purpose and then discarded. As Amy Laura Hall of Duke University writes in a *Christian Century* article, "To bring into being a human embryo solely in order to divide up its constitutive parts for research threatens fully to erode the sense that incipient human life is never simply, or primarily, a tool."[22] Rather than pursue cloning research, some observers urge that we focus upon critical public policy issues like the basic healthcare that many millions, perhaps billions, of people lack today.[23]

During the mid-1970's, I read an article that criticized organ transplants. I no longer own the magazine or recall the

> Bill McKibben's book, *Enough: Staying Human in an Engineered Age* (Owl Books, 2003), looks at technologies such as genetic engineering and robotics that pose real and potential threats to human well-being. As the title suggests, can or should we say "enough!" to scientific and technological development? When is the time when we should say "enough"? Read McKibben and consider some of the issues he raises.

author, but if I remember correctly, the author worried that transplants violated the integrity of our bodies and misused our God-created organs. The author feared that transplants departed from God's will. Today, organ transplants are much more commonplace and have prolonged and improved the lives of countless people. Will genetic research someday become as accepted and commonplace as organ transplants?

As Daniel McConchie, writing for the Center of Bioethics and Human Dignity, puts it, "In our utilitarian society, research science tends to plow ahead uninhibited by the constraints of moral principles and common sense. We must assume that if it can be developed, it will be . . . by someone, somewhere who sees some sort of gain in doing so. . . . [W]e need clear and vigorous debate in this country (and around the world) on what constraints ought to be placed on these new abilities."[24]

Christians can certainly contribute to the public debate (and there is a tremendous amount of theological writing on these subjects). This is not to say that Christians should approach these difficult and complex issues with Scriptures used as discussion-ending slogans. But Christians can productively bring scriptural truths, theological convictions, and sincere insights to discussions of medical research and treatment. Ideally, Christians can avoid the liberal-conservative labeling, vilification, and divisiveness so prevalent in contemporary discourse and, instead, approach public debates with a sense of genuine love (1 Thessalonians 5:12-15). The "image of God" is an excellent theological concept concerning human identity, dignity, and interdependence with other people and other life.

We're Dust, Yet Much More

You've heard the expression, "He's a real piece of work." The phrase comes from Shakespeare's *Hamlet*, in a declaration of how paradoxical are humans.

> What a piece of work is a man! how noble in reason! how infinite in faculty! in form and moving how express and admirable! in action how like an angel! in apprehension, how like a god! the beauty of the world! the paragon of animals! And yet, to me, what is this quintessence of dust?[25]

Clearly we are a special thing in the world: the most skilled and advanced species, capable of wonderful and terrible things; yet we are dust. The Hebrew word for "human being" is actually *'ādām*, which derives from the word *'ădāmâ*, or "ground." Similarly, the Latin word *humus*, or "soil," is related to our English word "human."[26] We are "flesh," to use Paul's image (Romans 7:13–8:17), stuck in our sin and unable to please God. Yet God provides us an abundance of grace for our benefit (8:10-11).

God's grace touches us very personally in times of illness. The advancements of modern medical science provide new areas for understanding—and new areas that God blesses with grace.

Closing
Close by reading together Genesis 1:26–2:3.

For Further Reading
Bodies and Souls, or Spirited Bodies? by Nancey Murphy (Cambridge University Press, 2006).

Enough: Staying Human in an Engineered Age, by Bill McKibben (Owl Books, 2003).

Fearfully and Wonderfully Made: A Policy on Human Biotechnologies, from the National Council of Churches USA, 2006; accessible at: http://www.ncccusa.org/pdfs/BioTechPolicy.pdf.

From Cells to Souls—and Beyond: Changing Portraits of Human Nature, edited by Malcolm Jeeves (Eerdmans, 2004).

Modern Physics and Ancient Faith, by Stephen Barr (University of Notre Dame Press, 2003).

The Politically Incorrect Guide™ to Science, by Tom Bethell (Regnery Publishing, Inc., 2005).

Science and Providence: God's Interaction With the World, by John C. Polkinghorne (Templeton Foundation Press, 2005).

Whatever Happened to the Soul? Scientific and Theological Portraits of Human Nature, edited by Warren S. Brown, Nancey Murphy, and H. Newton Malony (Augsburg Fortress Press, 1998).

Notes

[1] *Whatever Happened to the Soul?: Scientific and Theological Portraits of Human Nature*, edited by Warren S. Brown, Nancey Murphy, and H. Newton Malony (Augsburg Fortress Press, 1998); pages 227–28.

[2] *The Physics of Star Trek*, by Lawrence M. Krauss (Basic Books, 1995); pages 68–69.

[3] From "What Does It Mean to Be Human? Another Chapter in the Ongoing Interaction of Science and Scripture," by Joel B. Green, in *From Cells to Souls—and Beyond: Changing Portraits of Human Nature*, edited by Malcolm Jeeves (Eerdmans, 2004); pages 186, 196.

[4] Green, "What Does It Mean to Be Human?" in *From Cells to Souls—and Beyond: Changing Portraits of Human Nature*; pages 196–97. See also "'Bodies—That Is, Human Lives': A Re-Examination of Human Nature in the Bible," by Joel B. Green, in *Whatever Happened to the Soul?: Scientific and Theological Portraits of Human Nature*; page 157.

[5] Green, "'Bodies—That Is, Human Lives,'" in *Whatever Happened to the Soul?: Scientific and Theological Portraits of Human Nature*; page 172.

[6] From Paul Tillich's *Dynamics of Faith*, as quoted in *The Shaping of Modern Christian Thought*, by Warren F. Groff and Donald E. Miller (The World Publishing Company, 1968); page 424.

[7] Green, "What Does It Mean to Be Human?" in *From Cells to Souls—and Beyond: Changing Portraits of Human Nature*; pages 179–82.

[8] See the essay, "The 'Nature' of Desire," by Rachel Berman, specifically "Part 4: Genes, Altruism, and Evolution," written for Bryn Mawr College; accessible at: http://serendip.brynmawr.edu/bb/berman/.

[9] See "Faith and Medicine: A Growing Practice," by Jay Copp, in *St. Anthony Messenger*, March 2000; accessible at: http://www.americancatholic.org/Messenger/Mar2000/feature2.asp.

[10] "Faith-Based Medicine," by Raymond J. Lawrence, in the *New York Times*, online version, April 11, 2006.

[11] "Religion and Medicine: Why Faith Should Not Be Mixed With Science," by Richard P. Sloan and Larry VandeCreek, in *Medscape General Medicine*™, online version, August 4, 2000.

[12] From "In This Study, Prayers Aren't the Answer," by Jeremy Manier, in the *Chicago Tribune*, online edition, March 31, 2006.

[13] From "Ministries of Health: Our Tradition and Our Challenge," by Deborah White, in *Interpreter*, January-February 2006; pages 14–15.

[14] *The Hidden Face of God: How Science Reveals the Ultimate Truth*, by Gerald L. Schroeder (Touchstone, 2001); pages 194–95. See also the session, "A Map of Life," by Paul E. Stroble and Timothy L. Bryan, in *FaithLink*, Vol. 6, No. 12, July 23, 2000; pages 1–2.

[15] Stroble and Bryan; pages 1–2.

[16] Stroble and Bryan; pages 3–4.

[17] See the National Institutes of Health's webpage on "Stem Cell Information"; available at: http://stemcells.nih.gov/info/faqs.asp. See also the article, "Somatic Cell Nuclear Transfer (Therapeutic Cloning)," from the website of the Association of American Medical Colleges (AAMC, 1995–2007); available at: http://www.aamc.org/advocacy/library/research/res0003.htm.

[18] *The Politically Incorrect Guide™ to Science*, by Tom Bethell (Regnery Publishing, Inc., 2005); pages 125–28.

[19] Bethell; pages 136–37.

[20] UMNS "Close Up" report, "Stem Cells Raise Questions About Ethics, Healing," by Julie K. Buzbee, August 23, 2002 (United Methodist Communications, 2005); accessible from: http://archives.umc.org/umns/news_archive2002.asp?ptid=2&story={1B0CBD36-A605-4D88-89F7-1FF039C14DD4}&mid=2399.

[21] "U.S. Falling Behind in Embryonic Stem Cell Research," from U-M and Stanford University news services; accessible from *The University Record* online at: http://ipumich.temppublish.com/cgi-bin/pr.cgi?/~urecord/0506/Apr10_06/07.shtml.

[22] "Price to Pay: The Misuse of Embryos," by Amy Laura Hall, as it appeared in *The Christian Century*, June 1, 2004.

[23] This point is discussed in an article by William Bole, see especially the subhead, "Critics Say Cloning Misuses Health Resources"; accessible from the website of the General Board of Church and Society of The United Methodist Church at: http://www.umc-gbcs.org/site/apps/s/content.asp?c=fsJNK0PKJrH&b=860861&ct=1130973.

[24] From "Biotech Debates Are Being Muddled by the Media," by Daniel McConchie, for the Center for Bioethics and Human Dignity, April 5, 2001; accessible at: http://www.cbhd.org/resources/biotech/mcconchie_2001-04-05_print.htm.

[25] From *Hamlet*, by William Shakespeare, Act II, Scene II (Shakespeare-literature.com, 2003); accessible at: http://www.shakespeare-literature.com/Hamlet/7.html.

[26] "The Book of Psalms: Introduction, Commentary, and Reflections," by J. Clinton McCann, Jr., in *The New Interpreter's Bible*, Vol. IV (Abingdon Press, 1996); page 1099.

CHAPTER 7
FAITH AND SCIENCE TOGETHER

Focus: This session looks again at the relationship of religion and science and considers how we read the Bible in our age of science.

Gathering

Share refreshments with other group members at the beginning of this session. Read together Matthew 6:25-34. Jesus compares the natural world to our lives; why do we worry so much? Observation of nature can redirect our thinking from anxieties to God's help. Pray for God's guidance in ways we can strive "for the kingdom of God and his righteousness" (verse 33).

How Should They Interact?

I began this book with my daughter's comment, "'Religion and science'? That's a weird combination!" Hopefully at this stage of our study together, you find the combination less weird.

However, the relationship between religion and science will continue to be debated. Public issues like medical research, the environment, public school curriculum, and other topics show no sign of abating. In this book, I've discussed a variety of scientific and religious topics so that we can approach contemporary issues with greater understanding.

In Chapter 1, we briefly saw that science and religion can interact in different ways: by conflict, independence, integration, dialogue.[1] Of these, conflict is perhaps most easy to understand. You hear more about conflict between science and religion than about the other ways they interact. Whenever you hear of the case of Galileo, whenever you hear about school boards questioning the teaching of evolution,

> As stated in Chapter 1, Ian Barbour, in his book *When Science Meets Religion: Enemies, Strangers, or Partners?*, shows how conflict, independence, dialogue, and integration function in areas of religion and science. Also, find some of John Polkinghorne's books in which he discusses the interrelationships of science and religion. After experiencing this study, what potential do you see in each of the ways of interaction?

you get the impression that science and religion will always be at loggerheads.

Conflict as a form of interaction is necessary in a free society. As John Green of the Ray C. Bliss Institute notes, "Americans live in a very scientifically- and technologically-sophisticated society. Americans are also very spiritual and religious, and our society is increasing in religious diversity. My European colleagues ask me, puzzled, 'How can you Americans be so scientific and yet so religious?'" He notes that conflicts of worldviews and basic assumptions are inevitable in such a complex society.

Many of us dislike conflict in our personal lives. Religion suffers from a stereotype that conflict is always "resolved" through authoritative leaders or imperious appeals to Scripture (like the bumper sticker I once saw,

> What value, if any, do you see in conflict between religion and science?

which read: "God said it, I believe it, that settles it."). But conflict can be a very healthy thing when differences among people are clarified and a new consensus results. As we have seen, religion and science do not have to be in *essential* conflict.

Religion and science also interact through their independence. The late paleontologist and widely-read author Stephen Jay Gould published *Rocks of Ages*, in which he argues that religion and science are two legitimate fields of inquiry that should not interfere with each other. He calls them "nonoverlapping magisteria" (abbreviated NOMA).

Gould's term "nonoverlapping" may be confusing; he doesn't mean that science and religion are totally separate, but rather that they teach different things with different methods. The two fields can certainly speak to each other about mutual concerns. In his words, "The dialogue will be sharp and incisive at times;

> Do you think the independence of science and religion help or inhibit faith development? Why? Explain.

participants will get riled up, as a blessed consequence of our unextinguishable [sic] human nature; but respect for legitimate differences, and a recognition that full answers require distinctive contributions from each side, should maintain a field of interest, honor, and productive struggle."[2]

Still another form of interaction is dialogue. Certain recent theologians, like Wolfhart Pannenberg, Karl Rahner, and David Tracy, have explored ways that science and religion can speak to each other. A few science authors, notably Rachel

> What do you see as the benefits of dialogue as a way of interaction between science and religion?

Carson and Loren Eiseley, have used religious imagery in their discussions.[3]

A fourth way that religion and science interact is through integration. Ian Barbour, who has written much about the interrelation of science and religion, notes that both the "theology of nature" and "process philosophy" fall under this category.

> What comes to mind for you as you think about the integration of science and religion?

Barbour cites Pierre Teilhard de Chardin, a Roman Catholic paleontologist, as an example of integrating science and religion.[4]

Which of these four means of interaction holds the most promise for you? I prefer the way of dialogue. In our present time, public discourse can be divisive and winner-take-all. But I see benefit in upholding the integrity of scientific method on one hand and theological reflection on the other so that both are recognized as legitimate areas of thought, yet both can speak to each other and contribute mutual insights.

What if religious people heeded the concerns of scientists about the importance of rational argument, especially when the religious start to do hurtful things in the name of religion? What if scientists heeded the

Zygon®: Journal of Religion & Science has been published since 1965 and is the journal of The Institute on Religion in an Age of Science. Check to see if your nearest college library has copies of *Zygon®*, or obtain back issues through interlibrary loan. Leaf through the articles, which are scholarly and academic, and see what interesting topics are covered.

The Gifford Lectures, a prestigious lectureship sponsored by the University of Edinburgh, was established in 1888 to promote natural theology and the knowledge of God. According to their website, http://www.giffordlectures.org, the 2006–07 lectureship of Simon Conway Morris concerns evolutionary theology and religion.

concerns of sincere religious people about certain experiments, especially when long-range moral issues seem to be ignored in the name of progress? As we saw in Chapter 1, some of our most pressing contemporary concerns are scientific ones: global warming, public school science curriculum, and stem-cell research. Such concerns would be profitably addressed through a relationship of positive dialogue.

Faith and Reason

The theologian Paul Tillich (1886–1965) has helpful thoughts about this subject:

There is no conflict between faith in its true nature and reason in its true nature. . . . Reason gives the tools for recognizing and controlling reality, and faith gives the direction in which this control may be exercised. . . . Reason is identical with [our] humanity. . . . the basis of language, of freedom, of creativity. It is involved in the search for knowledge, the experience of art, the actualization of moral commands. . . . If faith were the opposite of reason, it would tend to dehumanize [us].[5]

Tillich writes that there is no essential conflict between faith and reason; for if we elevate the cognitive part of reason above our other functions, faith becomes a "lower form of knowledge." He argues that the truth of faith is different from the truth of science, history, and philosophy. However, faith, too, is guided by the cognitive aspect of our minds.[6]

Scientific truth finds its truth in the "adequacy of the description of the structural laws which determine reality" and the verification of these through experiments. "Every scientific truth is preliminary and subject to changes both in grasping reality and in expressing it adequately."

But, Tillich continues, "It is a very poor method of defending the truth of faith against the truth of science, if theologians point to the preliminary character of every scientific statement in order to provide a place of retreat for the truth of faith."[7]

Tillich notes further, "Science has no right and no power to interfere with faith" and vice versa. "On the other hand, if representatives of modern physics reduce the whole of reality to the mechanical movement of the smallest particles of matter, denying the really real quality of life and mind, they express a faith, objectively as well as subjectively"—a faith, that is, that the universe is only a "meaningless mechanism. In opposing this symbol of faith Christian faith is right." Tillich similarly notes that people who interpret Genesis as science interfere with science; and also that "a theory of evolution which interprets man's descendance [sic] from older forms of life in a way that removes the infinite, qualitative difference between man and animal is faith and not science."[8]

Will our modern scientific worldview ever seem like a quaint stage in human history? It doesn't seem likely. In his classic work, *The Varieties of Religious Experience*, William James predicted the possibility of such a change. He wrote in 1902,

> Do you think science will become an "eccentricity"? Why or why not?

> The divorce between scientist facts and religious facts may not necessarily be as eternal as it at first sight seems. . . . [for] the rigorously impersonal view of science might one day appear as having been a temporarily useful eccentricity rather than the definitely triumphant position which the sectarian scientist at present so confidently announces it to be.[9]

Lingering Dilemma

Several years ago I wrote my first book, a history of my hometown when it was the Illinois state capital in the early 1800's.[10] I used research methods to analyze historical data, and then I wrote a book that was peer reviewed and published. It has been used by both history buffs and academic historians.

As a religious person, I believe that God is active in the human historical process, as depicted in the Bible. At no time was I tempted to introduce religious interpretations into my history book. It was beyond my research and knowledge to determine how God acted among persons and events in the nineteenth-century time period that I studied (though I do believe that God worked in the lives of those persons). Nor am I considered an inadequate or "superstitious" historian because I have strong religious views.

Yet, when it comes to religion and the naturalistic sciences, we raise these kinds of expectations. Perhaps that is because science (unlike academic history) so much pervades our lives, and the truths of science seem different from the truths of Scripture. Events that are presented in the Bible as factual cannot be explained by science and often fly in the face of scientific truth.

But are we forcing the Bible to be something that it's not? In his best-selling book about the Bible, *The Good Book*, Peter J. Gomes asks, "What *does* the Bible say about science?" And he answers, "Nothing." He continues, "To impose the constraints of science upon the Bible is to force it into a role for which it was never intended, and to which without violence to author, text, and reader, it cannot be adapted."[11]

Sciences Affects Our Bible Reading

During my seminary program, I was privileged to study briefly with the American theologian Hans Frei (1922–1988). In his book *The Eclipse of Biblical Narrative*, Frei notes that prior to the 1700's, Christians read the Bible in a very realistic way. "The words and sentences meant what they said, and because they did so they accurately described real events and real truths. . . . Other ways of reading portions of the Bible, for example, in a spiritual or allegorical sense, were permissible, but they must not offend against a literal reading."[12]

Do you have a Bible story or passage with which you strongly identify, or which is a personal favorite? How is that story or passage "about you"?

In addition, these readers understood the Bible stories to be about them. When we read, for instance, about the broken-hearted publican whom God forgives, that story is our experience, too. What Frei calls the "figural interpretation" of the Bible is a way of placing oneself in the biblical stories.[13]

But as Frei notes, in the eighteenth century the literal-figural meaning of the Bible began to break down as people became concerned with more "scientific" questions. Are the Bible stories historically true? Did they "really" happen? Is the Bible a unified text or is it a compilation involving many different authors, editors, and theological viewpoints and agendas? How can we believe the biblical miracles when they are depicted as violations of natural laws and scientific physical principles? Can we get a better grasp of scriptural meaning when we analyze its philological and historical aspects than from a literal reading? The result, writes Frei, is a greater variety of tools to interpret the Bible but also a "distancing" of the earlier sense of reading the Bible in a pre-scientific, literal, and figurative way.[14]

While the earlier theologians saw faith and reason as complementary (Chapter 3), some thinkers closer to our own time have interpreted Scripture in such a way to accommodate the truths of science. For instance, philosopher David Hume (1711–1776) and theologian Friedrich Schleiermacher (1768–1834) in different ways emphasized the experiences that give rise to religious ideas, rather than the literal meaning of Scripture. Johann Herder (1744–1803) emphasized the linguistic and cultural experiences "behind" Scripture, taking a historical approach to its study. David Strauss (1808–1874) took a very non-literal view of Scripture, applying science to the reading of Scripture. For Strauss, the biblical miracles have mythological aspects.[15]

On one hand, a "scientific" way of reading the Bible is enormously helpful. Today, we can appreciate the many aspects of the text: its literary genres, styles, and traditions. We can come closer to understanding the authors' intentions. We can understand the Bible in its historical, cultural, and philological dimensions.

On the other hand, because of our knowledge of science, we question the literal sense of the text. Did Jesus *really* walk on water? Did the sun *really* stop in the sky at Joshua's command? Did the Red Sea *really* part? Such things are

> How do you read and interpret the Bible? Are you more at home with a "scientific" reading or a "literal" reading? What do you see as the strengths and weaknesses of these ways of reading and interpreting?

scientifically impossible; yet these things are recorded in Scripture, crucial both for the memory of God's mighty acts and the guarantee that God continues to act in wonderful ways on our behalf.

Peter Gomes writes that the German and American traditions of "higher criticism" of the Bible (that is, the study of the sources and the literary and historical roots of the biblical texts) are valuable but very far from the traditions of "black preaching," which is "overwhelmingly narrative." He continues, "Black preaching endeavors to remove as many barriers between the thing preached and those to whom it is preached as quickly as possible, so that the 'objective' story becomes with very little effort, 'our' story, or 'my' story." Thus "black preaching" is both literal and figural to use Hans Frei's terms, but without being fundamentalist. Gomes holds that "African Americans who read and heard the Bible did not stop to ask if it was literally true, inspired, and inerrant, for they knew that on the authority of their own experience as a people troubled, transformed, and redeemed."[16]

Making the Bible Scientific

Some of us feel that the Bible's authority needs to be vindicated by science. Or, to put it another way, science will eventually vindicate the truth of Scripture if we give science enough time; and meanwhile, we rejoice when scientific discoveries "prove" biblical material.

Peter Gomes writes that "it is little short of amazing how widespread and virtually unchallenged is [the] theory of the supersession of secular knowledge, that the Bible and nearly all that comes from it is left only for those who do not know any better." Furthermore, many, many people believe that "the Bible's credibility has been destroyed by science . . . therefore, only science can restore the Bible's credibility."[17] We hear news stories about the identification of the Bethlehem star, the remains of Noah's ark, and archaeological discoveries which verify that David, Jesus, and other biblical figures really lived—as if the truth of the Bible were suspect and therefore we need scientific evidence to "really" prove it true. We read magazine articles about areas of reconciliation and interconnection between science and religion. All these reflect

> All churches use science and technology, from printed books to telephones to microphones and more. The Internet is an increasingly popular means for congregations to reach out to people. Some congregations employ economic marketing methods for outreach, while others gauge the strength of their church through scientific quantification. Do you think congregations ever rely too much upon scientific and technological methods? Is there a line between the methods that churches use (which could work in any organizational setting, with or without God's help) and the power of the Holy Spirit?

interest that science can verify biblical truth, or at least dovetail with biblical truth.

Stephen Jay Gould complains that both science and religion are diminished by forced connections. In one *Newsweek* article that he references, the two natures of Jesus were said to parallel the dual nature of light (it can behave as either waves or particles).[18] Gould is defending the integrity of science rather than affirming religious doctrine, but his point is well taken. Do we need quantum theory to prove that Jesus is Lord? While analogies and connections may be interesting, do they unintentionally misrepresent what religious truth is?

Interpretation

As I said earlier, even the most conservative among us do not take the Bible as a 100%-literal account. Take the beautiful verse Isaiah 55:12, "For you shall go out in joy, and be led back in peace; the mountains and hills before you shall burst into song, and all the trees of the field shall clap their hands." Surely the prophet was not reporting a literal event that happened, no more than the poet spoke literally about his beloved, "Your eyes are doves behind your veil" (Song of Solomon 4:1). The Bible is filled with poetry, similes, and metaphors; and as Peter Gomes points out, we do violence to the text when we insist that the Bible become a scientifically-perfect account.

The Bible is also filled with diverse accounts of the same events. There are two Creation stories, for instance (Genesis 1:1–2:3 and 2:4-24), and two stories of God's command to Noah (6:19-22 and 7:1-5). Pick up a copy of *Gospel Parallels*, by Burton H. Throckmorton, Jr. (Thomas Nelson, Inc., 1992); and see how the details vary among the Synoptic Gospels (Matthew, Mark, and Luke). If our faith *requires* a 100%-literal Bible, then we'll spend a great amount of time being very defensive about the truth of the Bible and, I speculate, we'll never convince people who approach the Bible from a more scientific framework.

But as noted in Chapter 2, the Holy Spirit is the chief way by which the Bible becomes alive and real to us. The Spirit opens us to the truth of the Bible, helps us understand and interpret the Bible, convinces us of its truth, and leads us into a relationship with God. The Spirit does not destroy our reason, nor asks us to suspend our reason in order to have faith. The Spirit works with our reason in order to prove the Bible to us— and to others.

We interpret the Bible not as a letter-perfect text but as a lived experience made possible by the living Christ. As Chuck Barnes puts it, *"Uninterpreted and wooden,* revelation loses its lifeblood. Beliefs become rigid and unquestioned; absolutist dogma leads to atrocities done in the name of *my particular* God. *Interpreted and lived,* revelation leads to a lifetime of devotion and a pouring out of one's love."

Dan R. Dick writes about a scientist who disliked religion, who told him, "If science taught me anything, it is to trust my senses and to test every thesis. Religion has nothing to offer on this front." (Recall that in Chapter 1, Dick said most scientists he has met do struggle with issues of faith.) Dick responded to the scientist, "You reject religious experience based on what tests?" The person responded that she had none, so Dick offered her to "follow a spiritual discipline of prayer, meditation, and fasting for four weeks and record observations of the experience in a journal, as you would observe a culture in a lab."

The woman followed his advice. Later she told him,

> I cannot say I experienced God, but I experienced something. In addition to focus, calm, and clarity, I felt *something*—something undefined, but very real, very compelling. Whatever it is—God, soul, or a chemical reaction, I don't know—but I am going to pursue it. . . . I don't know whether to thank you or curse you. This whole exercise calls into question what I 'know.'[19]

Believing Thomas

That brings me to the most notoriously "scientific" person in the Bible: Thomas the apostle. What a bum rap he has gotten! We know him as "Doubting Thomas" and apply his name to skeptical people. In the story about Thomas (John 20:24-29), Jesus seems to scold him: Thomas wanted proof of the Resurrection—observable verification—but Jesus told him that faith is a better way. Can you find a better anti-science-proof-text than that?

Read John 20:24-29. When have you reacted as Thomas did to what his friends told him? What connections do you see between Thomas and a "scientific" point of view? How did Jesus respond to him? How do you think God responds to our need for "proof"?

But as my pastor, Jim McClaren, recently portrayed in a sermon, we can read the story in another way. If you have lost a close friend, as I have, you'll understand Thomas' sadness and confusion. In his grief, Thomas (who is laudably faithful and bold in John 11:16) needed something to help his faith; and Jesus—generous Savior that he is (Ephesians 3:20)—gave him three things. First, Jesus gave him special attention, separate from the other disciples. Second, Jesus didn't begrudge Thomas the proof that he needed: first-hand confirmation of his resurrection. Third, Jesus gave him *another* proof to help his faith. Thomas had not accepted the testimony and experience of his friends concerning the Resurrection, but Jesus assured him that such testimony was a reliable proof for his faith.

We can trust Jesus' assurance for our own faith. *You and I* are the ones God blesses (John 20:29). None of us will touch Jesus' skin and wounds. But we can experience his love and grace in our lives. We can trust the experience of our Christian friends when our own faith needs assurance. We can experience his help in the many aspects of our lives. We can live in a scientific world and trust that Jesus is as real to us as he was for his disciples.

In his first letter to the Corinthians, Paul cautions the church not to lose the sight of the important things (1:18–2:5). The Corinthians dispute about who is wisest among them, but they forget how to love. Paul reminds them: you can have all the answers and all the religious wisdom of the world, but if you lack love, you have nothing at all (13:2).

One way to grow in love is to own, cherish, and live the stories of the Bible as if they were about us. And in an important way, they are.

A Spirit of Love

Imagine a magazine cover story: "SECRET OF THE UNIVERSE DISCOVERED." That would be an exciting story!

Actually, we've known the secret of the universe for over three thousand years. It is God's love. And among other Scriptures, three psalms provide us with this faith-knowledge. First, read Psalm 19:1-4a.

> The heavens are telling the glory of God;
>> and the firmament proclaims his handiwork.
> Day to day pours forth speech,
>> and night to night declares knowledge.
> There is no speech, nor are there words;
>> their voice is not heard;
> yet their voice goes out through all the earth,
>> and their words to the end of the world.

Writing in *The New Interpreter's Bible*, J. Clinton McCann, Jr., reflects on this psalm. "In essence, Psalm 19 affirms that love *is* the basic reality. . . . [T]he God whose sovereignty is proclaimed by cosmic voices is the God who has addressed a personal word to humankind—God's *torah.* Furthermore, this God is experienced ultimately by humankind not as a cosmic enforcer but as a forgiving next of kin! God is love, and love is the force that drives the cosmos."

McCann writes, "Psalm 19 is not anti-science, but it does offer a view of the universe as something more than an object to be studied and controlled. To be sure, nature is not divine, but it is incomprehensible apart from God. In some sense, nature 'knows' God (verse 2), and thus it can proclaim God's sovereignty."[20]

> One of the themes that we've seen throughout this study is the interconnectedness of the universe. While scientists seek a unifying theory, other scientists point out the connection of ecological health with human health, the interrelationships of organic life through similar DNA patterns, the relationships within the expanding universe, and other connections. Do you see possibilities of science and religion cooperating on issues of the interdependence of nature? Why or why not?

Next, read Psalm 136:3-7.

O give thanks to the Lord of lords,
    for his steadfast love endures forever;
who alone does great wonders,
    for his steadfast love endures forever;
who by understanding made the heavens . . .
who spread out the earth upon the waters . . .
who made the great lights. . . .

About this psalm, McCann writes,

According to Psalm 136, steadfast love characterizes the attitude of God toward the whole cosmos, including the earth and all its features and all its creatures. There can be no more profoundly good news than this—that God's attitude toward the world and God's motivation for action are summarized by steadfast love. . . . As Exod[us] 34:6-7 makes eminently clear, steadfast love inevitably involves God's grace. Thus Psalm 136 ultimately affirms that the origin, continuity, and destiny of the cosmos are dependent upon the grace of God.[21]

Finally, read Psalm 104:24, 33-34.

O LORD, how manifold are your works!
In wisdom you have made them all;
     the earth is full of your creatures. . . .
I will sing to the LORD as long as I live;
     I will sing praise to my God while I have being.
May my meditation be pleasing to him,
     for I rejoice in the LORD.

The whole psalm praises God for creation and sustenance. From the stars and moon, to the earth's mountains and trees, to the small creatures, God's works and wisdom are manifold. As McCann puts it,

The poet who wrote Psalm 104 was an environmentalist. . . . The psalmist's awareness was grounded . . . not in a knowledge of physical sciences. . . . [but] in *theology*. The psalmist was convinced of the profound interdependence of air, soil, water, and all living things, because he or she believed that *everything* derived from and was ultimately dependent upon God.[22]

Though their methods and conclusions differ, perhaps science and religion will someday find enduring partnership in two places where they profoundly agree: the interdependence of all things and the importance of serving humankind.

Closing
Light a candle and think about these things:

    God's love for human beings
    God's love for all creation
    God's compassion for sinners and those who suffer
    God's righteousness that holds us accountable
    God's justice that calls us to serve one another
    God's care for the tiniest organisms
    God's care for the planet Earth
    God's providence that extends to the farthest stars

Conclude by reading together 1 Corinthians 13.

Notes

[1] *Science and Theology: An Introduction*, by John Polkinghorne (Fortress Press, 1998); pages 20–22. See also *Religion and Science: Historical and Contemporary Issues*, by Ian G. Barbour (HarperSanFrancisco, 1997); pages 77–105.

[2] *Rocks of Ages: Science and Religion in the Fullness of Life*, by Stephen Jay Gould (Ballantine, 1999); page 211.

[3] Barbour; pages 90–98.

[4] Barbour; pages 98–105.

[5] From Paul Tillich's *Dynamics of Faith*, as quoted in *The Shaping of Modern Christian Thought*, by Warren F. Groff and Donald E. Miller (The World Publishing Company, 1968); pages 418–19, 422.

[6] Groff and Miller; page 422.

[7] Groff and Miller; page 422.

[8] Groff and Miller; page 423.

[9] *The Varieties of Religious Experience: A Study in Human Nature*, by William James (The Modern Library, 1936); page 491.

[10] *High on the Okaw's Western Bank: Vandalia, Illinois, 1819–1839*, by Paul E. Stroble (University of Illinois Press, 1992).

[11] *The Good Book: Reading the Bible With Mind and Heart*, by Peter J. Gomes (HarperSanFrancisco, 1996); pages 317–18.

[12] *The Eclipse of Biblical Narrative: A Study in Eighteenth and Nineteenth Century Hermeneutics*, by Hans W. Frei (Yale University Press, 1974); page 1.

[13] Frei; pages 2–3.

[14] Frei; page 6.

[15] Frei; pages 137, 151, 183–89, 236–39, 298–99. For more on Strauss, see "David Friedrich Strauss: Miracle and Myth," by Marcus Borg, in *The Fourth R*, Vol. 4:3, May/June 1991 (Polebridge Press, 1991); accessible at: http://www.westarinstitute.org/-Periodicals/4R_Articles/Strauss/strauss.html.

[16] Gomes; pages 340–41.

[17] Gomes; pages 314–15.

[18] Gould; pages 215–16.

[19] "Facing the Wrong Way—God, Darwin, and Being Too Smart for Our Own Good," by Dan R. Dick; accessible from the website of the General Board of Discipleship of The United Methodist Church at: http://www.gbod.org/TextOnly.asp?item_id=8729.

[20] "The Book of Psalms: Introduction, Commentary, and Reflections," by J. Clinton McCann, Jr., in *The New Interpreter's Bible*, Vol. IV (Abingdon Press, 1996); page 753.

[21] McCann, Jr.; page 1225.

[22] McCann, Jr.; page 1099.